GW01071991

A Cat's Soliloquy

Learning Japanese through Poetry

Mitsue Jimi

ORIGINAL WRITING

Cover Photography and *Kestrel of Bahji* painting by
Conrad Reina
Origami art: http://niko-niko-nihongo.com

978-1-908477-28-6

A CIP catalogue for this book is available from the National Library.

Published by ORIGINAL WRITING LTD., Dublin, 2011.

Printed by CLONDALKIN GROUP, Clonshaugh, Dublin 17

前書き

　この本の詩は私が１９９２年から２０１０年まで書き溜めたもので、それはまるで私の独り言のようなものです。それでも、何か、あなたに通じるものがあって、このそよぐ風のようにあなたと共に存在することが出来たら、非常に幸いです。

　世界中の多くの人達に読んで頂く為に、英語の翻訳を付けました。特に日本語を勉強している方々のお役に立てるように、全ての漢字に読み仮名が付けてあります。私の詩は韻律や定型の規則とは無縁ですので、散文詩の類になりましょうか。

　前置きはさておき、どうぞ、私の詩をお楽しみ下さい。

　最後になりましたが、出版にあたり、ご協力頂きました飯島美希様、コンラド・リナ様、アシュリンゴ様、大島御夫妻、出版社の皆様、深く御礼申し上げます。

　　　　　　　　２０１１年５月　　　　自見　良津枝

我が国　日本

我が故郷　福島の復興の為に

IV

PREFACE

The poetry in this book spans the years from 1992 through 2010 and can be likened to my soliloquy. However, there might be something contained within the poems which speaks to you. I would be very happy if my poetry would accompany you, like this wind, which is breathing softly.

I have attached an English translation because I would like many people all over the world to read my poetry. To this end I have included Hiragana for all the Kanji in order to be more readily accessible for Japanese language learners.

I would like to thank Ms. Miki Iijima, Mr. and Mrs. Ooshima, Mr. Conrad Reina and Ms. Aisling Reina for the help they have given me. Also thanks are due to the publishing staff.

My poetry is a kind of prose because it makes its own rules of rhythm and pattern. Please enjoy my poetry!

Mitsue Jimi

For my country, Japan
For my hometown, Fukushima

May 2011

セレクション

SELECTED POEMS

PAGE 2 TO 65

セレクション

SELECTED POEMS

下関の鯨

私は下関の鯨
今は丘の上にいるが
昔はよく関門海峡を
行ったり来たりしたもんじゃ

私が泳ぐと
外国の大きな船でさえも
嵐のように揺られ
のんびり浮かんではいられなかった
慌てふためく様を見るのは
とても楽しいものじゃった

今は　毎日　落ちる夕日を丘から眺め
灯るポチポチとした
街の明かりを見ながら
日本も平和になったものだ
と、思うばかりじゃ

2002.12.22

2

A Whale in Shimonoseki

I am a whale in Shimonoseki.
Though I am on a hill now,
I often used to swim around the Kanmon Strait.
When I swam
Even foreign ships were rocked,
As if a storm had come,
And they could not float leisurely.
I would really enjoy watching those who were very upset.
Now I view the setting sun everyday.
I am just thinking that Japan became peaceful,
Looking at the lights,
Which are like speckles in the town.

22 December 2002

猫の独り言

にこは猫
猫は猫なりに時を過ごす
英語のレッスンに行ったり
日本語のレッスンに行ったり
掃除をしたり
洗濯をしたり
買い物をしたり
遊んだり

今年はあっという間だったニャー
と満足気に笑みを漏らし

いくら波乱万丈でも
最後に良かった
幸せだと思えることが大切なのだ
来年も良い年になるといいニャー
と独り言を言った

2008.12.20

4

A Cat's Soliloquy

Niko is a cat.
This cat spends her time living at her own pace.
She goes to English lessons and Japanese lessons,
She cleans her house,
She washes her clothes,
She goes shopping and plays...
She smiles with satisfaction, saying:
"This year has passed very quickly, *nyaa*."
And she also whispered:
"It's very important for us
To have such an ending that
We can feel happy about
However checkered our life may be.
I hope that we will be happy next year
As well, *nyaa*."

20 December 2008

デジモン挽歌

節分の豆の数
年の数
おもむろに出した数
１６個
それでも　お前が食べる分には
余ってしまう
不意に襲ったお前の死

生きよう　生きよう

節分の豆
お前の分まで食べて
お前の分まで生きてみせよう

１９９８.２.４

6

ELEGY FOR DEGIMON

The number of beans for *Setsubun*.
The number of your age.
There are sixteen beans that I took out
Without intending to.
But they will be too much for you.
It was a sudden death, which took you.
I'll live, I'll live.
I will eat your beans for you on *Setsubun* and
Try living for you.

                                    4 February 1998

窓

小さい窓からは小さい空しか見えない
年々　私の部屋は
だんだん薄暗くなってきている
だんだん小さく　仕舞いに
ポチッとついている
オレンジ色の豆電球は希望かな
部屋の窓も
年々　小さくなっていく
空も　小さくなっていく
向こうの空を飛ぶ鳩の存在も
知らない
流れる雲について
何処から来て　何処へ行くのかさえも
見えない
ただ　分かるのは
風が吹いていることだけ
小さい窓からは小さい空しか見えない

1998.7.25

8

A WINDOW

We can only see a small sky
From a small window.
My room is getting dimmer gradually every year.
Is the orange coloured light bulb which
Became smaller and ended up being a tiny light
My only hope?
The window of my room is growing smaller
Every year.
The sky is also shrinking.
I can't know of the existence of a white dove
That is flying in the other sky.
As for clouds that are floating,
I can't see even where they come from or
Where they are going.
I only know that
The wind is blowing.
We can see only a small sky
From a small window.

25 July 1998

缶の中の金魚たち

一歩が死んだ
青木が死んだ
鷹村が死んだ
木村が死んだ

お前たち、1日1匹ずつ
死んじゃうんだね
パン粉は嫌いだったのかい
もっと酸素が欲しかったのかい
缶の中は嫌だったのかい

一歩が死んだ
青木が死んだ
鷹村が死んだ
木村が死んだ

本当は名前が嫌だったのかい
ごめんね　お前たち

１９９２

GOLDFISH IN A CAN

Ippo died.
Aoki died.
Takamura died.
Kimura died.
You guys have died one by one, one each day.
Didn't you like bread crumbs?
Do you want more oxygen?
Did you dislike being inside a can?
Ippo died.
Aoki died.
Takamura died.
Kimura died.
Did you hate your names, in fact?
I'm sorry, guys.

1992

秋の夕暮れ

白い半月の空を飛ぶよ
この帽子
その帽子
あの帽子
トンボは止まって伝えてくれる

秋が来たよ
鈴虫が鳴くよ
ススキが揺れるよ
空が高いよ

向こうの田んぼを見てごらん
夕日が照らして綺麗だね
秋の夕暮れは淋しいから
もう帰ろう
風に吹かれて
もう帰ろう

2002.10.13

Autumn Twilight

They fly in the sky of a white half-moon.
This cap,
That cap,
The cap over there.
Dragonflies tell us, landing on our heads:
"Autumn came."
"Bell-ringing crickets will sing."
"Japanese pampas grass will wave."
"The sky is high."
Look at the rice paddies over there.
They are so beautiful
Because the twilight sun lightens them.
Let's go home,
As the autumn dusk makes us feel lonely.
Let's go back home,
Blown by the wind.

13 October 2002

太陽

太陽の光ってすごいよ
眩し過ぎて　目を開けてられない
電車で逃げても　逃げても
追いかけてくるんだ
やる気をいっぱい出してくれる
うん、生きようって　強く思うんだ
ショボン・・・と、してても
こんなに照らされちゃ
笑うしかないね
だから　ちょっと照れ笑いで
変な顔になっちゃったよ

1996.4.12

14

THE SUN

Sunlight is amazing.
I can't keep my eyes open
Because it's so bright.
Even though I run away, on and on
On a train,
It chases after me.
It makes me very energetic
With a strong will to live.
I was depressed
But I had no choice except to smile
Because I was brightly illumined
By the sunlight.
So, I smiled bashfully a little
With a funny look on my face.

12 April 1996

幸福な夢

幸せ？私にとっての幸せとは、、、、、、

家族が１つであること
遠く離れていても　心は１つ
近くにいても　バラバラじゃ意味がない
簡単だけれど　難しい夢
ずっと　私は夢見てる
幸福ってそんなものかも知れない

１９９２

A HAPPY DREAM

My happiness?
What my happiness is...
A situation in which my family is always together.
Our hearts are always together
Even though we are far away from each other in different places.
There is no point in being together
Unless our hearts are together.
It's a simple dream,
But it's also a difficult dream.
I have dreamed of it for a long time.
Happiness may be like this.

1992

２２日の夜

台風が去った後の空は
純粋な夜空
東京で初めて見る　綺麗な星空
強い風が　一切を
吹き飛ばしたのだろう
東京での私の心は
スモッグがかかった空

台風よ　来い
もう一度　綺麗な星を見せておくれ

１９９６．９．２６

The Night of the Twenty-second

The sky after a typhoon is a clear night sky.
It is a beautiful starry sky in Tokyo such as
I have never seen before.
It seems that a strong wind cleared everything.
My heart in Tokyo is like a smog-filled sky.
Come on, typhoon!
Please show me the beautiful stars
Again.

26 September 1996

かざぐるま

倒れた自転車はかざぐるま
夜が来るのは遅くなって
朝が来るのは早くなって
ほのかな春の香りの風が
かざぐるまを回す

いいや　騙されんぞ
昨夜は粉雪が舞っていた
ほら　吐く息もこんなに白い

それでも　もうすぐ春が
訪れる予感がするのです

1997.2.19

Pinwheels

Bicycles that have fallen over look like pinwheels.
Night falls late and morning visits early.
The wind, which smells faintly of spring
Spins the pinwheels.
No, I won't be deceived!
A fine snow was dancing last night.
Look, my breath is also white.
In spite of those things,
I foresee that spring is coming soon.

19 February 1997

Ｄｉｎｇｌｅ　Ｂａｙの巨人

Ｄｉｎｇｌｅ　Ｂａｙに浮かびながら
いつも昼寝をしている巨人がいます。

夜、暗くなって、街の灯りが消えてから
巨人は起きて、陸に上がって来ます。

いくつもの畑を
のっし、のっし、跨いで
あるＢ＆Ｂに来ました。
そして、窓を覗き込んで言いました。

明日がどうなるか、なんて分からない。
ただ、幸せな明日を迎える為に、
今日、一生懸命頑張るだけさ。
人の人生は辛くも、簡単にもなる。
それを選ぶのは自分。
一度、それを選んだら、
毎日が楽しいと思えるように
自分を導かなければならない。
また、それが出来なくても
がっかりすることはないんだよ。
また頑張れば良いのだから。

そう言って、海に帰って行きました。

　　　　　　　　　　　　　２００８．１０．２７

22

A Giant in Dingle Bay

There is a giant who always takes a nap
Floating in Dingle Bay.
He gets up and comes to the land
After it becomes dark and
The lights in the town go off at night.
He strode over patches of land: nosshi nosshi
And came to a B&B.
Next he looked inside a window and said:
We don't know what will happen tomorrow.
We should just work hard today
To welcome happiness tomorrow.
Our life can be both hard and easy.
It's you who makes the choice.
Once you make your choice
You have to lead yourself
To be able to feel happy everyday.
Also, you don't have to be disappointed
Even if you can't do so.
Because there won't be a problem if you try again.
He said this and went back to the ocean

27 October 2008

Ｌｕｃｋｙはキュッと言った

Ｌｕｃｋｙはキュッと言った
小さい命　守れなくて　ごめん
お前の幸せを保障してやろうなんて
出来なかったよ
分かっていたことなのに
辛い思いさせて　ごめん

お腹いっぱい　食べさせてあげたかったな
お腹いっぱい　向日葵の種
食べさせてあげたかったな
うんと　うんと広い大地で
花と一緒に
回る落ち葉と一緒に
遊ばせてあげたかったな

川も海も雨も知らずに
死んでしまった
澄み切った冬の夜空には
キランと星が光ることも
風がヒュウとなって囁くことも
知らずに
春には薄桃の桜が木にぶら下がって
ユラユラ揺れるんだぞ

なのに　お前は笑って
ほんとに笑って
私に挨拶をしてくれるのかい

１９９８．２．２４

Lucky said "Kyu"

Lucky said "Kyu".
I'm sorry I am not able to protect your
Little life.
I wanted to secure your happiness
But I couldn't.
I had known that.
I'm sorry I made you miserable.
I wished I had let you eat as much as you liked.
I wished I had let you eat a lot of
Sunflower seeds.
I hoped that I had let you play with
Flowers and fallen leaves, which danced
Together on the extremely vast field.
You passed away without knowing
Rivers, the sea and rains,
Without knowing that stars shine
In the clear winter night sky and
That winds whisper, making a noise, hyuu.
Do you know that pale pink cherry blossoms
Sway, depending from trees, in spring?
In spite of this,
Will you smile and greet me?

24 February 1998

泣いて帰った帰り道

蝸牛を踏んだ
蝸牛は死んだ

道が暗かったし、
泣いていたから、分からなかったの

蝸牛は言った
どんなにショックで辛くても
死ぬわけじゃないから
大丈夫だよ

蝸牛は逝った
私は生きている
蝸牛は身をもって教えてくれたんだね

2005.9.30

26

I Returned Home Crying

I stepped on a snail.
The snail died.
I didn't see you
Because the street was dark and
I was crying.
The snail said:
"Don't worry because you won't die
No matter how much you are shocked
And disappointed."
The snail passed away.
I am still alive.
He taught me through his death.

30 September 2005

あの夏へ帰ろう

あの夏へ帰ろう
まだ何も考えず
まだ何の不安や責任もなかった
あの夏へ帰ろう

夏の暑い日
私は自分の人生を歩き出した
それは今ここへ来る為の
入り口だった
何も考えず　扉を叩いた
何も知らず　扉を開いた

もう長く歩き過ぎて
入り口は見えなくなってしまった
もう帰れない

帰れないと分かりつつ
また思ってしまう
あの夏へ帰ろう

2000.8.3

28

LET'S RETURN TO THAT SUMMER

Let's return to that summer!
Let's go back to that summer
When I hadn't thought anything yet or
I hadn't any anxiety or responsibilities
At all…yet!
On that hot summer day
I started waking on my own.
It was the entrance for me to come here now.
I knocked at the door without thinking.
I opened the door with my innocence.
I can no longer see the entrance
Because I walked away so long ago.
I can't return there anymore.
I know that I can't return
But I wish again that I could.
Let's return to that summer.

3 August 2000

スリランカのヤモリ

ヤモリはじっとして何を考えているのかな
銀歯が取れて、どうしようと不安になったり
沢山虫が飛んで来て、うんざりしたり
スクライルがカカカと鳴いて
怖い思いをしたりするのかな

もし、私がヤモリなら
沢山の虫はご馳走で
壁に這いつくばって、ひっそりと
人間に見つからないように
柱の陰に身を隠すだけ

2003.6.24

A Gecko in Sri Lanka

I wonder what a gecko is thinking
While not moving.
I also wonder if the gecko can be scared
By a squirrel that cries: ka ka ka
Or annoyed by many flying insects
Or become anxious about the solution of
A silver tooth that came out.
If I was the gecko,
Many insects would be my feast and
I would only hide myself behind a pillar
Sticking out of the wall, quietly,
So as not to be found by humans.

24 June 2003

夢から覚めた時のように

夢から覚めた時のように
全ては一瞬のうちに消えてしまう

昨日までの生活
楽しい笑い声
苦々しく思ったこと
パンの焼ける匂い
あの道　あの低い空

全てはブラックホールに吸い込まれて
何事もなかったかのように
再び始まる
そう　夢から覚めた時のように
２ヵ月もの間　私は眠り続け
今　目覚めたかのように

　　　　　　　　　２０００．１２．９

32

It Seems Like When I Awake from a Dream

Everything disappears in a moment,
As if I just awoke from a dream.
Life until yesterday,
Happy laughter.
Things that disgusted me.
The smell of toast.
That street, the low sky of England.
All is swallowed up in the black hole and
My daily life restarts
As if nothing happened.
It seems as if I awoke from a dream.
It seems like I woke up now
After I had slept
For two months.

9 December 2000

三日月

真っ黒の空に
のどかに煌々と浮かぶ三日月
それは冬の田舎の象徴だ
でも　もう後一時間半もすると
もっと　取って付けたような
貧弱な都会の三日月に変化する

同じ月でも全く違うように見えるのは
見る場所が違うからなのか
私の精神状態が違うからなのか

また　当分の間
月を見る余裕すらなくなってしまうのか
それでも　私の胸の中に
今日　見た美しい三日月の記憶をとどめておいて
辛い時に思い出すことにしよう

　　　　　　　　　　　１９９７．１１．４

A CRESCENT

It's a crescent moon, which rises pastorally,
Brightly in the black sky.
It's a symbol of the winter countryside.
Yet, after one hour and a half
It will change into a poor, urban crescent moon,
Like an artificial one.
I feel it is a different moon
Even though I am looking at the same moon.
Does it depend on the vantage point from which I observe it?
Or does it depend on my mental state?
I wonder if I will be too busy even to look
At the moon for a while again.
However, I will keep my memory of
This beautiful crescent moon I looked at today
In my heart and remember the moon
When life is hard for me.

4 November 1997

蝉（せみ）

ミーン　ミーン
儚（はかな）い夏（なつ）の声（こえ）

たったの　ほんのわずかな命（いのち）
一体（いったい）　誰（だれ）が定（さだ）めたの
心（こころ）は何（なに）を思（おも）っているの
花（はな）は来年（らいねん）もまた咲（さ）くけれど
その声（こえ）を聞（き）くことは出来（でき）ないね
そういうのを運命（うんめい）というの
明日（あした）　私（わたし）はどうなるか分（わ）からない
でも　花（はな）も私（わたし）も希望（きぼう）はあるのに
夏（なつ）の声（こえ）は儚（はかな）い

ミーン　ミーン
儚（はかな）い

ミーン　ミーン
儚（はかな）い

１９９６.８.２６

CICADAS

Miin, miin.
Short-lived voice in summer.
A mere tiny life.
Who on earth decided it?
What are they feeling in their hearts?
Though flowers boom next year again,
And I can see it,
I can't hear the voice again.
Should I call it fate?
I don't know what will happen to me tomorrow,
But there is hope both for me and for flowers.
The summer voice is frail.
Minn, minn.
It's fragile.
Minn, minn.
It's fragile.

26 August 1996

親切なＳｅａ　ｇｕｌｌさん

授業をサボった午後
日焼けを楽しみながら
昼寝をしていると・・・

コツ　コツ　コツ

誰かしら
私のブーツを叩くのは
あなたは海のＳｅａ　ｇｕｌｌさん
私を呼びに来てくださったのね
クラスメイトの代わりに

　　　　　　　　　　　１９９５．３．１３

38

A KIND SEAGULL

One afternoon when I skipped a class,
When I was taking a nap
Enjoying getting a suntan....
Kotsu, Kotsu, Kotsu,
Who is rapping upon my boots?
You are Mr. Seagull from the sea.
You called to me
Instead of my classmates.

13 March 1995

笑顔でいてね My Sister

優しい希子ちゃん とっても大好き
可愛い希子ちゃん 幸せでいてね

だけど そんなに優しくしないで
私は返すことが出来なくて
胸が苦しい
希子ちゃん これから 幸せでいてね
嫌なことが起こらないといいな
悲しいことが起こらないといいな
私はそう思うことしか出来ません

優しい希子ちゃん 優しい希子ちゃん
あなたの 妹 で良かったと思うの
幸せになってね

                                    1992

Please be Happy and Smile, my Sister

Kind Kiko-chan, I really love you.
Pretty Kiko-chan, please be happy.
But please don't be so kind.
I feel guilty because I can't return your kindness.
Kiko-chan, please be happy in the future.
I hope bad things won't happen to you.
I hope you won't see sadness.
I can only hope these things for you.
Kind Kiko-chan, kind Kiko-chan,
I am so lucky that I am your sister.
Please be happy forever.

1992

愛しい我が家

２２年前　我が家に小さな女の子が生まれた
少女はすくすくと育った

そこには喜びがあった
そこには悲しみがあった
そこには幸せがあった
そこには不安があった

好きだった
大嫌いだった

今はもう戻れない光景
だけど　あぁ、もう一度戻りたい
愛しの我が家

１９９２

42

MY SWEET HOME

A little girl was born to our family twenty-two years ago.
The girl grew up healthily.
There was joy there.
There was sorrow there.
There was happiness there.
There was anxiety there.
I loved my home.
I hated my home.
The scene I can no longer return to now.
Oh, however, I'm eager to return there.
It's my sweet home.

1992

豆電球

オレンジ色の
古く懐かしい
惨めな
でも　温かい
幸せな
静かな夜の光

私はどうなってしまうのだろう
お父さん　お母さん
私はどうなってしまうのでしょうね

２００１．１．２９

A Miniature Bulb

It is orange colored,
Old, familiar,
Miserable,
But it is a warm and happy
Light from a silent night.
What's going on with me?
Father, Mother,
What will happen to me?

29 January 2001

治療法

痛みに弱い私は
嫌なことを忘れるように
水中に潜って
ひたすら
眠る　眠る　眠る・・・

いっそ　このまま死んでしまえたら
と思ってみても
それは出来ない
大好きなあなたに会えなくなってしまうから
大好きなあなたに会うことを夢見て
ひたすら
眠る　眠る　眠る・・・

素敵な明日を夢見て
眠る　眠る　眠る・・・

２００６.２.２７

CURE

I who am vulnerable to pains
Sleep, sleep, sleep entirely
Under the water
In order to forget things which bother me.
I can't do so,
Even though I think that
It would be nice if I died
In this situation now.
Because I wouldn't be able to see
You, who I really love.
I sleep, sleep, sleep,
Dreaming of a wonderful tomorrow.

27 February 2006

無題

まだ幼く小さい頃に
戻りたいと思うことがありますか
私は強く強くそれを願うのです

絶対叶うことのないことと知りながら
タイムマシーンでもなければ
戻ることなんて出来ないと分かっていても
もう　あの時代の　あの場所の
あの家族はないと知りながら
今がどんなに幸せであっても
あの頃を思えば
どんな楽しいことも　成功も
ちっぽけなものに見えてしまうのです

あの平和で幸福であったあの頃を思えば
いいえ　決して平和でもなく
幸福であったともいえないかもしれない
なのに　あの頃と同じような風が吹く度
空がゴォーと音をたてる度
私の記憶はあの頃に戻り
強く強く幼少の頃に戻りたいと願うのです

しかし　もし神様が 私 の願いを叶えて下さって
戻れたとしても　ただ戻っただけならば
同じことを繰り返し　大人になった 私 は
再び同じことを願うことになるでしょう
今の脳みそを持って戻ったとしても
あの頃とは違い
別の歴史を歩むことになるでしょう
今の 私 のこの願いは
全ての結果が出た後に思うことであり
もっと最悪の結果を招くことにもなりかねません

風に吹かれる度
空の音を聞きながら
私 は絶対叶うことのない願いを
繰り返し　繰り返し　考え
それが 私 の人生というのならば
何と 儚く薄暗い人生であるといえましょう
私 に感情 というものがある限り
私 はこの願いを永遠に抱き続け
自分の一生を終えるのではないかと思います

１９９７.１.７

49

Untitled

Do you sometimes think that
You would like to return to your childhood?
I really really hope to return,
Although I know that dream will never come true.

Unless we have a time machine or something,
It's impossible to return.
I also know that the family I knew
At that place, in those days,
Doesn't exist anymore.
Yet, any joy and success that I have these days seem to be
But tiny things,
No matter how happy I am now
When I remember that moment,
When I think of those days when
I was in that peaceful and happy world.

No, I might not be able to say that
It was entirely peaceful and happy,
But my memories of those times returns, and
I wish to return to my childhood with all my might
Each time I feel that same wind
Blowing as before,
Each time I hear the sound
The sky makes.

However, I would repeat the same
Things again as I grow older and
End up wishing for the same things again,
If I just returned to my childhood,
Thanks be to God.
Even if I returned to my childhood as
I am now,

It would be different,
And would happen differently.
It would lead to a worse outcome.
This current wish of mine is the wish
I made after all the consequences of past actions
Had happened and gone.

Each time the wind blows on me,
I hear the sound of the sky and
Repeatedly wish the same wish
Which will never come true.
If this is to be my life,
I will say that life is fragile and dim.
I think that I will hold onto this wish forever
Until I finish my life,
As long as I have emotions.

7 January 1997

桜の言うこと

桜新町の桜はユッサユサ
ユッサユサ　ユッサユサと
揺れながら
重い頭を垂らして
通りの人並みを眺めている

この時代の人間は
何故　あぁも　くたびれているのだろう
どうして　こんなに
しかめっ面をしているのだろうか

桜の木達は
隣同士で話している
そして

人間達よ
空を眺めよ　透明な風の音を聞き
本当に美しく大切なものを悟れよ

と語り掛ける
しかし　人間は気付かない
夢中でセカセカと歩いているのだ

1999.4.17

Messages from Cherry Blossoms

Cherry Blossoms trees in Sakurashin-machi are
Weeping with their heavy heads and
Viewing people on the street,
Swaying: *yussa yusa, yussa yusa, yussa yusa.*
Why do the people of this age look so tired like that?
Why do so many people frown with faces like this?
Cherry Blossom trees are talking next to each other.
And they try to speak to us.
Dear people,
Look at the sky!
Listen to the sound of the lucid wind
And sense what really beautiful and important beings they are!
However, people don't notice these things.
They are too busy walking hurriedly without looking up.

17 April 1999

桜の傘

雨　しとしと
雨　しとしと
セットした髪が乱れます

ちょいと
この傘にお入りなさいな
こちらの傘にも
こっちにも・・・

どうもありがとう
お陰で濡れずに済みました

優しい桜新町の桜の木
誰も持っていない
大きなピンクの傘でした

２００２.４.１１

54

CHERRY BLOSSOM UMBRELLA

Rain: *shito, shito.*
Rain: *shito, shito.*
My hair was just done, and now it's getting tousled and wet.
"Excuse me,
Why don't you come under this umbrella?"
"Come under this umbrella as well."
"This one too."
Thank you very much.
I didn't get wet, thanks to you.
Gentle cherry blossom trees in Sakaurashimmachi.
They were big pink umbrellas such as no one else has.

11 April 2002

セブンアップ

缶の中に　Ｌｕｃｋｙちゃんがいる
多分　もうすぐ一年になるから
私に会いに来てくれたのだろう
キュッキュッと鳴く声は
とても懐かしい

透明な炭酸水は　生命の水
生まれては消えて
Ｌｕｃｋｙちゃんも
生まれては消えて
死んでしまった

Ｌｕｃｋｙちゃんはプチッと生まれ
パチンッと消えた

缶の中にｌｕｃｋｙちゃんがいる
沢山いる

1999.2.19

56

SEVEN-UP

Lucky-chan is inside a tin can.
Maybe he came to visit me
Because one year will soon have passed.
His voice: kyu kyu, is very familiar to me.
Transparent soda water is the water for life.
They were born and then disappeared.
Lucky-chan was also born and then died.
Lucky-chan was born: puchi, and then
Disappeared: pachin.
There are a lot of Lucky-chans
Inside the tin can.

19 February 1999

ある日　電気を直して思ったこと

ある日　電気を直して思ったこと
虫の死骸がいっぱいあって

ギャーッてなって

ほこりまみれになって

汗まみれになって
手が真っ黒になって

こんなこと
他の大人がやってくれればいいのにって
ちょっと思って

それでも
再び明かりが点いた時は
嬉しくて

エヘンッとなって

生きるって大変なんだなぁー

1999.9.1

My Thoughts after I fixed a Light on the day

There is a thing that I thought
When I fixed the light on the day.
There were a lot of insect carcasses, and
I was frightened by them.
I was covered with dust and sweat,
My hands were very dirty,
I wished a little that other adults could help
Me for tasks such as these;
Yet, I was very happy and proud of myself
When the light was on again.
It's really tough to stay alive.

1 September 1999

太陽の光と幸せ

人は太陽の光の中にいるとき
それを当たり前と思う
夜が来て、朝が来るのは
当然と思っている

太陽の光が無くなったとき
人は
あの時、自分は幸せだったのだと気付く

どんな状況でも
決して最悪ではないのだと思っている人は
果たして
どのくらいいるのだろうか

2005.2.13

Sunlight and Happiness

When we are in sunlight,
We feel that it is natural.
We are thinking it is natural that
Morning should come after night.
When we lost the sunlight,
We realized that
We had been happy at the time when the sun shown.
How many people are thinking that
It's not the worst
No matter what the situation is?

13 February 2005

日本を離れる時

春には桜が咲き
夏には蝉の音
秋には鈴虫
冬には雪が舞い
そう、ここは日本

大好きな人の笑顔が
沢山あるここを離れて
私は一体
何を求めているのでしょう

究極の幸せって
一体何なのでしょうね

分からない、分からない
うっすらと遠くに見える光
その先に何があるのか
ただ、知りたいだけなんです

2004.3.30

When I Leave Japan

Cherry blossom trees bloom in spring.
Songs of cicadas in summer.
Bell-ringing crickets in autumn.
Snow dances in winter.
Yes, here is Japan.
I'll leave here, where there are the many smiles
Of the people who I love.
Where on earth will I go?
Father, Mother,
What in the world am I asking for?
What is the supreme happiness?
I don't know, I don't know.
I just simply want to know
What is there ahead of the faint light
Which I can see far away.

30 March 2004

幸せなどんぐり

公園を急いで歩いている時
どんぐりが私の肩を叩いた

「そんなに急ぐなよ！
　景色がこんなに綺麗じゃないか。
　もっと　人生を楽しめよ！
　気付いていない素晴らしい物が
　まだ沢山あるじゃないか。」

疲れて家路に辿り着いた時
小さなどんぐりが
ひょっこり顔を出して、言った

「お疲れ様、
　もう　ゆっくり休んでいいんだよ。」

「ありがとう。
　君のお陰で、幸せな気分になったよ。」

　　　　　　　　　　　２００６.１０.２６

Happy Acorn

When I was walking quickly in a park,
An acorn tapped my shoulder.
"Don't hurry like that!
The scenery is so beautiful here, isn't it?
Enjoy your life more!
There are many wonderful things that
You haven't noticed yet!"
When I became tired and returned home,
The little acorn turned up unexpectedly and said:
"Hard work!
You can take your time and relax now!"
"Yes, thank you. I became happy, thanks to you."

26 October 2006

<ruby>年代<rt>ねんだい</rt></ruby><ruby>順<rt>じゅん</rt></ruby>

COMPLETE COLLECTION OF POEMS IN CHRONOLOGICAL ORDER

愛しい我が家

２２年前　我が家に小さな女の子が生まれた
少女はすくすくと育った

そこには喜びがあった
そこには悲しみがあった
そこには幸せがあった
そこには不安があった

好きだった
大嫌いだった

今はもう戻れない光景
だけど　あぁ、もう一度戻りたい
愛しの我が家

１９９２

MY SWEET HOME

A little girl was born to our family twenty-two years ago.
The girl grew up healthily.
There was joy there.
There was sorrow there.
There was happiness there.
There was anxiety there.
I loved my home.
I hated my home.
The scene I can no longer return to now.
Oh, however, I'm eager to return there.
It's my sweet home.

1992

幸福な夢

幸せ？
私にとっての幸せとは､､､､､､

家族が１つであること
遠く離れていても　心は１つ
近くにいても　バラバラじゃ意味がない
簡単だけれど　難しい夢
ずっと　私は夢見てる
幸福ってそんなものかも知れない

１９９２

A HAPPY DREAM

My happiness?
What my happiness is...
A situation in which my family is always together.
Our hearts are always together
Even though we are far away from each other in different places.
There is no point in being together
Unless our hearts are together.
It's a simple dream,
But it's also a difficult dream.
I have dreamed of it for a long time.
Happiness may be like this.

1992

虫の音を聞きながら

夜は暗い
とても暗い
家々の明かりが沢山灯ろうとも
私は自分の明かりを探し歩く
どこまで行けば良いのだろう
一体何を探し求めているのだろう
ふと気が付くと　今ここに私がいる
そして　また明日へ向かって
生きねばならないのだ

　　　　　　　　　１９９２

WHILE I'M LISTENING

The night is dark.
Very dark.
I walk and seek for light
In spite of many lights shining in houses.
I wonder how far I must go.
I wonder what I'm looking for.
I suddenly realise I'm here now.
And I have to live for tomorrow... again.

1992

秋の夜の独り言

人間は勝手だ
とても我儘な動物だ

馬はもっと生きたかったかもしれない
走れなくても生きたかったかもしれない
きっと　どこかで恨んでいるかもしれない

そう思ったら　胸がつまって
釜飯がのどを通らない
大好きなトリ唐でさえも、
あまり食べられなかった
なのに、何故だろう
秋祭りの金魚すくいで
弱っている小さな出目金をすくってしまったのは

人間は矛盾だ
そして、私もその一人なのだ

１９９２

74

A Thought one Autumn Night

Human beings are egoistic.
Very selfish animals.
The horse may have wanted to live longer.
Even though she couldn't race anymore,
The horse may have hoped to live.
Probably she is plotting against humans somewhere.
I was so moved to tears when I considered these things
That I had no appetite for kamameshi.
I couldn't eat even my favorite tori-kara
Rather than kamameshi.
Yet I wonder why
I scooped up a tiny weak goldfish at an Autumn Festival.
Human beings are paradoxical.
And I'm one of them.

1992

父と私の夏の思い出

暑い電車に揺られながら
私はあなたのことを考えています
ガタガタ音をたてている窓は
光に反射して　とても眩しく
あの夏を思い出させます

楽しかったですね　猪苗代湖
綺麗ですね　心の中で言ってみます
ボートの上の無邪気な笑顔は
水面より眩しくて
私は目を細めます

また行きましょう
また行きましょう
キラキラした夏の思い出は
どんな宝石よりも　とても大切な
大切な記憶なのです

$$1992$$

76

My Memory of a Summer with my Father

On a hot day being shaken by a train,
I'm thinking of you.
A loose window reflects light,
And it's very dazzling.
It reminds me of the summer
We enjoyed together.
It was fun in Inawashiro-ko, wasn't it?
"How beautiful!" I thought.
As your innocent smiles on the boat were
More sparkling than the water,
I squinted my eyes.
(I smiled to you too.)
Let's go again!
Let's go again!
This brilliant summer is
More important and precious to me than
Glittering gems.

1992

缶の中の金魚たち

一歩が死んだ
青木が死んだ
鷹村が死んだ
木村が死んだ

お前たち、1日1匹ずつ
死んじゃうんだね
パン粉は嫌いだったのかい
もっと酸素が欲しかったのかい
缶の中は嫌だったのかい

一歩が死んだ
青木が死んだ
鷹村が死んだ
木村が死んだ

本当は名前が嫌だったのかい
ごめんね　お前たち

１９９２

GOLDFISH IN A CAN

Ippo died.
Aoki died.
Takamura died.
Kimura died.
You guys have died one by one, one each day.
Didn't you like bread crumbs?
Do you want more oxygen?
Did you dislike being inside a can?
Ippo died.
Aoki died.
Takamura died.
Kimura died.
Did you hate your names, in fact?
I'm sorry, guys.

1992

クリス

夜中　お酒を飲んでいると
クリスがそのビンの蓋で遊ぶ
騒がしいと怒られたので
おもちゃの猫じゃらしを揺らしてみた
知らん振りする
つまみのチーかまを食べていると
近寄ってきて鳴く
手に取ってあげようとすると
プイッとそっぽを向く
なんて我儘な猫なのだろう
だけど　そこが魅力的なのだ
私にはとても可愛いクリス

１９９２

CHRIS

Chris played with the bottle cap.
While I was drinking beer at midnight.
I tried swinging a toy like a foxtail grass
Because I was told off: "Noisy!!"
She ignored both me and the toy.
She came closer and mewed
When I was drinking and eating a cheese-*Kamaboko*,
She turned away from me
When I was about to give her a piece by hand.
What a selfish cat she is!
However, that's her charm.
Chris, she is my darling.

1992

さくらの季節

さくらよ　さくら
綺麗な花よ　別れの花よ

嬉しい別れの時は
涙を流さず
さくらの花びらを
１つ２つ　頬に付けて
さくらの涙を流しましょう

さくらは私達の涙を知っている
幾度も幾度も花を咲かせて
私達の門出を祝ってくれる

さくらよ　さくら
優しい花よ

１９９２

Season of Cherry Blossoms

Cherry blossoms, cherry blossoms,
Beautiful flowers,
Farewell flowers.
If it's a farewell in which we are delighted,
Let's put one or two cherry blossom petals on our cheeks
Instead of teardrops.
Cherry blossoms know our tears.
They celebrate our departures
By blooming frequently.
Cherry Blossoms, cherry blossoms,
Tender flowers.

1992

記憶は私の財産です

記憶はとても素晴らしい
遥か遠く昔のことでも
昨日のことのように思い出せる

大きな階段を、手を取られ
一歩一歩　歩いたこと
座布団に寝かされ
秋のお庭を眺めていたこと
今だって白黒テレビを見ていても
色をつけることが出来る

記憶があるから
以前、見た記憶があるから
記憶はとても素晴らしい

1992

MEMORIES ARE MY WEALTH

Memories are amazing.
We can remember things from long long ago
As if they happened yesterday.
I remember walking down big stairs
Step by step, holding my parents' hands.
I remember being placed
On a flat cushion.
Looking at the Autumn garden.
I can put colours on it now
Thanks to memory,
Even if I watch a black and white tv show.
Because there is a memory of
What I watched before.
Memories are amazing.

1992

笑顔でいてね My Sister

優しい希子ちゃん　とっても大好き
可愛い希子ちゃん　幸せでいてね

だけど　そんなに優しくしないで
私は返すことが出来なくて
胸が苦しい
希子ちゃん　これから幸せでいてね
嫌なことが起こらないといいな
悲しいことが起こらないといいな
私はそう思うことしか出来ません

優しい希子ちゃん　優しい希子ちゃん
あなたの妹で良かったと思うの
幸せになってね

1992

PLEASE BE HAPPY AND SMILE, MY SISTER

Kind Kiko-chan, I really love you.
Pretty Kiko-chan, please be happy.
But please don't be so kind.
I feel guilty because I can't return your kindness.
Kiko-chan, please be happy in the future.
I hope bad things won't happen to you.
I hope you won't see sadness.
I can only hope these things for you.
Kind Kiko-chan, kind Kiko-chan,
I am so lucky that I am your sister.
Please be happy forever.

1992

帰り道

秋の夕暮れ　とても冷たい
私の心は　とても寒い
独りぼっち　独りぼっち
おいしいシチューの香り漂うあの家は
私の家かな？
フラフラ　フラフラ歩いても
私の家はありません

独りぼっち　独りぼっち
私の心は　とても淋しい
秋の夕暮れ　とても悲しい

1992

88

On My Way Home

Autumn twilight.
It's very chilly.
It's very cold in my heart.
By myself, by myself.
I wonder if that house with the smell of delicious stew is my house.
My house is nowhere
Even though I walk around unsteadily.
By myself, by myself.
My heart is very lonely.
Autumn twilight.
My heart is very sorrowful.

1992

静かな夜の公園で

時々　お月様とお話したよ
公園の大きいブランコに乗ってさ
お月様は優しく話しかけてくれるんだよ
今日１日あったことを話すんだ
笑いかけると
笑ってくれた　キラキラって
帰る時　いつも
「淋しくなったら、またいらっしゃい」って
言ってくれたよ
だから　お月様って好きなんだ

１９９２

In a Silent Night Park

I talk with the Moon sometimes,
Riding on a big swing in a park.
The Moon spoke to me gently.
I talked about what had happened today.
When I smiled at her,
She also smiled at me radiantly.
When I would leave for home,
She always would say,
"Come and visit me again when you are lonely."
So I like the Moon.

1992

雨の歩道橋

今日は大雨　とっても大雨
複雑な雨　悩む雨
空にも 心があったなら
そんな気持ちになった時
雨を降らせるのかもしれないね
八木田橋で行列を作った黒アリが
七色のこんぺいとうを
運んでいたよ
そんなことを思い出す
今日は雨の日

１９９２

Rainy Pedestrian Bridge

It's raining heavily today.
It's a downpour.
Complicated rains.
Suffering rains.
If the sky also had a heart
And had mixed feelings,
The sky might create rain.
A procession of black ants were
Carrying seven-colour Kompeitou
On the pedestrian bridge.
The rain brought back the old memory.
It's raining heavily today.

1992

大きな夕日に照らされて

顔がオレンジ色になってきた
船のあっち側とは反対に
ここは明るい
私達の笑顔があるから
寒い風なんて　気にしない
5人でいれば　十分心が温かい

あの島　あの船　あの断崖
全てがオレンジ色に変わってく
船に続いたあの白い絨毯は
まだあるのだろうか

1993

I was Illumined by the Big Late Afternoon Sun

Our faces were becoming orange.
Our side was of the ship was bright
Because of our smiles.
And the brightness was the opposite of the other side of the ship.
We didn't mind the cold wind
As there were five of us and
Our hearts were warm enough.
That island, that bridge, that cliff,
They all were turning orange.
I wonder if the carpet which
Followed the ship is still there.

1993

グレーの休日

今日はグレーの休日
誰かに開けて欲しいと思った扉も開かず
フワフワと宙に浮いている
どこまでも果てしなく
グレーの雲は続いているのだ

強大な風が吹き
この雲を吹っ飛ばしてくれたらいいのに
チリヂリに飛ばしておくれ

願いは止めどなく繰り返されるが
やっぱり　今日はグレーの休日
そっと　小さくなってみる

１９９３

Day off in Gray

Today is my day off in gray.
A door that I hoped someone opened
Is still not open and
It's floating freely in the air.
Gray clouds spread limitlessly.
I wish a strong wind would blow away these clouds.
Blow them to pieces!
I constantly wish for this,
But today is my day off, after all.
I hold myself tightly, silently.

1993

参宮橋は春が似合う

春の日は桃色
夏の日は緑色
秋の日は黄色
冬の日は白色

自然の織りなす絨毯でございます
時には雨のカーテンで飾ってみせましょう
だけれども　何よりも
参宮橋には春が似合う

１９９３

SANGUUBASHI GOES WITH SPRING

Pink in spring.
Green in summer.
Yellow in autumn.
White in winter.
They are carpets woven by nature.
Let's try decorating with
Rain curtains sometimes.
In any case
Sanguubashi goes with spring
As well as anything.

1993

生きようとする気持ち

どんなに死にたい夜でも　朝は来る
あんなに流した涙は
一夜の嵐のように去っている

瞳を開けると　すがすがしい朝だ
黄金の光は　生命の力を与えてくれる
昨夜の嵐はどこへ行ってしまったのだろうか
私はこんなにも穏やかだ

言い表せない　この気持ち
誰に感謝すれば良いのか
ありがとう！

　　　　　　　　　　　　１９９４.2.7

I Feel Like Living

Darkness turns into dawn
No matter how much I want to die.
The tears I had shed with such profusion
Disappeared like a storm one night.
When I opened my eyes,
I felt the refreshing morning light.
The Golden Light can give us the power of life.
I wonder where last night's storm disappeared to.
I feel so calm now.
I can't express this feeling.
Who should I thank?
Thank you!

7 February 1994

失恋した君へ

君は何故泣くのか
輝かしい未来があるというのに
君は何故揺れるのか
素晴らしい明日が待っているというのに
君は何故止まろうとするのか
永遠の光はないというのに
悲しいのはほんの一瞬だけなのに
君は何故泣くのか

1994.4

To You, Broken-hearted

Although you will have
Your bright future,
Why do you cry?
Although you will see
Your wonderful tomorrow,
Why do you waver?
Although eternal light is not here,
Why do you intend to remain?
Even though there is no eternal love
From you to me, from me to you.
Despite merely a moment's sadness,
Why do you cry?

April 1994

赤いマニキュア

赤いマニキュア
私の心
赤いマニキュア
純粋な気持ち
赤いマニキュア
私の気合い
赤いマニキュア
情熱の赤の赤いマニキュアなのか
だけど　今日の赤いマニキュアは
みじめな赤色だった
赤いマニキュア
私にもよく分からない
赤いマニキュア
涙と一緒に混ぜたら
どんな色になるのかな
赤いマニキュア
私を慰めておくれ

１９９４.５.４

RED MANICURE

Red manicure.
My feelings.
Red manicure.
Pure heart.
Red manicure.
My spirit.
Red manicure.
Is it "red manicure" which means "passion red"?
However, today's red manicure was
Miserable red.
Red manicure.
I also don't know well.
Red manicure.
I wonder what colour it will be
If I mix it with my tears.
Red manicure.
Please console me.

4 May 1994

電子レンジ

電子レンジの中は幸せでいっぱい
オレンジ色が明るくて温かくって
くるくる回って楽しそう

ボンッ

幸せが崩壊した音かな
それとも　誰かがクラッカー鳴らした音かな
それなら　パーティーの始まりなのにね
　　　　　　　　　１９９４.５.２３

A Microwave Oven

There is plenty of happiness
Inside a microwave oven.
It seems so merry
As the orange light is bright, warm,
And moves in a spiral.
Bom!
Is it the sound of happiness collapsed
Or is it the sound of a cracker
Someone exploded?
If so, it will be the beginning of a party.

23 May 1994

川は生きている

汚い虹の川で
魚がいっぱい跳ねた
天気が良いので機嫌が良いのか

虹は歪んでは戻り
戻っては歪んできらめく

虹を歪ます程じゃない
小さな魚は足音でワッと逃げる
体も小さいけれど　結構
小心者なのかもしれないな

フジツボは干からびて死んでいる
と、見せかけて生きている
まるで忍者だ

あぁ、この川は生きているんだなぁ
童謡を歌って眺めていよう

1994.5.23

A River is Alive

Many fish jumped
In a dirty iridescent river.
I guess they are in a good mood
Because it's a sunny day.
The rainbow shined,
Expanded and contracted,
Then it contracted and expanded.
Fish, which are too small
To make the rainbow shake,
Swim away quickly because of footsteps.
They are tiny and
They may be fairly timid.
Barnacles are dry and seem to be dead.
But it's a pretence,
For they are still alive.
It seems as if they are ninja.
Oh, I feel this river is alive.
Let's view this river,
Singing nursery rhymes.

23 May 1994

あなたの汽車

今の私は　あの広い空を
フワフワと舞う風船のよう

汽車を途中下車しました
行く先、真っ黒な絶望が見えたからです
暗いトンネルはとても怖いのです
恐ろしい猛獣が現れて
　私を食べてしまうかもしれません
よく見ると、それは
　私を乗せている汽車だったりもするのです

だから　私は途中下車しました
明るいお花畑の道を選んだのです
1人でトコトコ行かなければなりません
幾たび　幾たび　後ろを振り返り
あの汽車を眺めるでしょう
その時　私は
あの地点がなかったらなと
思うに違いありません

　　　　　　　　　　1994.8.18

Your Steam Train

Now I'm like a balloon,
Fluttering in the vast sky.
I alighted from the train
In the middle of my journey
Because I foresaw in my destination
Dark despair.
The dark tunnel is so scary.
A vicious monster might appear
And eat me.
If I looked at it closely,
I might see that it was actually the train I was on.
So I stopped over,
I chose a bright path in flower gardens.
I have to go alone without dependence.
I'll look back at the train many times.
And then I must wish I hadn't passed the point.

18 August 1994

永遠の空は悲しくて

何のために生命が誕生し、
その一生を終えるのか
分からない

何ゆえに心ある者が
多くの命を奪ってまで生きるのか
分からない

何故　子孫を残さねばならないのか
分からない

どうして　そこに大宇宙があり
この地球があり
太陽の周りを回るのか
分からない

ある方はおっしゃった
長い年月を経て進化をはかり
いずれは何処かへ辿り着くのだろう
また　ある方はおっしゃった
神があるならば
きっと　神のいたずらであろう

そうであるかもしれないし
そうでないかもしれないし
私にはよく分からない

夏の終わりの青空が
果てなく広がる日は
こんな不思議が多い

　　　　　　１９９４.8.24

The Eternal Sky Makes Me Sad

I don't understand the reason why life appears
And then vanishes.
I don't understand why
Thoughtful people live
Even though they deprive many others of their lives.
I don't understand why
We have to leave offspring.
I don't understand why
There is a universe.
And why the Earth goes around the Sun.
A person once said
It'll reach somewhere someday
After long years of evolution.
Another person said

It must be God's mischief,
If God exists.
It may be like that or
It may not be like that.
I don't know for sure.
At the end of a summer day
When the endless blue sky stretches into eternity,
There are so many mysteries.

24 August 1994

２４の神秘的現象

あなたにはお分かりにならないかも知れませんが
女性の心と身体は密接に関係しているのです
今日　初めて気付いたような
もっと以前から知っていたのだけれど
改めて実感したような
そんな気分なのです

２４年目にしての感動です
深く落ち込み　暗く考え
物事を悪い方にしか考えられず
無性に死にたくなるのは
五感のせいだけではないのです
心と身体がつながっているからこそ
起こりうる神秘現象なのです
少なくとも私という女性はそうなのです

鳥肌が立つ程のこの感動を
あなたがお分かりにならないのは
とても残念としか言いようがありません
そして　これは特権であると考えて
笑みをこぼすべきなのでしょうか

　　　　　　　　　　　１９９４.８.２４

AGE TWENTY-FOUR:
A MYSTERIOUS PHENOMENON

You may not understand it,
But there is a close connection
Between a woman's heart and her body.
I feel as if I discovered it today
For the first time,
Or maybe I realised it again
Though I had known it before.
It's the impression I get, being now twenty-four years old.
It's not only because of the five senses
That we are deeply depressed,
Gloomy, negative, and eager to die.
It's a mysterious phenomenon
That is caused by the connection
Between a woman's heart and her body.
At least it's like that for me.
It's a pity that
You won't be able to understand
This earth-shattering revelation.
Should I think it's a female's privilege
And smile?

24 August 1994

雲　（パート１）

雲よ　雲
よくも　私の心地良いひと時の邪魔をしたね
お前は一体何処から来たのか
いつ　現れたのか
夢の中にいたので分からない

じぃーと睨めば　姿を隠す
大きな手をワッと広げて逃げていく者は
見ているだけで　面白く
モリモリと土が盛り上がるように
後ずさりして消えていく者は
初めての驚きとしか言いようがない
まるで　絵画のように美しく
なんて幻想的なのだろうか

まだ夢を見ているのかもしれない
仕方がない
雲よ　許してあげよう

１９９４.９.２６

CLOUDS, PART ONE

Hey, clouds!
How dare you disturb my snug time.
I don't know
Where on Earth you came from or
When you first appeared
Because I was dreaming.
When I glared at them, they went into hiding.
A cloud that is like a person who
Is running away
With his hands opened widely
Is so interesting to me,
Even though I am just an observer.
I can't help but feel surprised.
A cloud, like a person,
Draws away and disappears
As the Earth swells.
How beautiful and fantastic they are,
As if they are paintings.
I might be still dreaming.
Clouds, I am obliged to forgive you.

26 September 1994

雲　（パート2）

全体に薄く広がる雲
眩しい神の光を囲んで　輪の層を作る

今日は何か特別な日なのかい
あんなスピードで駆けて行く雲もいるじゃないか
きっと　空　果てしなく
呼び叫ぶのだろう

「今日は神の祭りの日だ
　今日は神の祭りの日だ」って

次から次とやって来る客
白い雲　黒い雲

いいねぇ　実に楽しそうだよ
美しいよ　あんた達
空に白いレースのカーテン掛けたみたいだ

　　　　　　　　　　　1994.9.26

CLOUDS, PART TWO

Clouds which flatly expand all over
Make layers of rings
Around God's light.
Is today a special day for something?
There is a cloud which flies
With deadly speed like that, isn't there?
I guess he must shout to the whole sky:
"Today is a feast!
Today is a feast!"
The guests come over
One after another:
White clouds, black clouds.
Very nice,
You look so merry.
You are so beautiful.
It seems like white lacy curtains
In the sky.

26 September 1994

九月二十日の月

ぼんやりと浮かぶ　優しい月
あの　おぼろなイーハートヴの月じゃなく
あの日　公園でお話した
お月様とも違う
月が変化をするように
人の心も変わるもの
何億光年の冷静な光に照らされて
人は心を落ち着けるのか
　心の嵐はまだ去らず
折角の満月も二重に見える
遠吠えをあげたい

　　　　　　　　　　　　１９９４.９.２６

THE MOON ON THE TWENTIETH OF SEPTEMBER

A tender moon dimly floats in the sky.
It's not the same as the pale moon in Ihatoobu.
It's also different from the moon
That I talked to in the park one day.
Our minds will change just as
The Moon changes its shape.
I wonder if people can compose their feelings
Through being illumined by the calm light
Of the moon whose light comes from so far away.
The storm in my heart hasn't gone,
And I see even a precious full moon double.
I want to howl.

26 September 1994

フローリングに響く泣き声

あぁ　なんと可哀想なことをしたのだろう
あぁ　なんと愚かなことをしてしまったのだろう

賢治の心に近づく為に
少しの間　菜食主義になろうと
決めたばかりなのに

あぁ　蚊が泣いている
あぁ　恨めしそうに泣いている

血を少し分けてあげるだけなのに
ほんのちょっぴりかゆいだけなのに

羽音が気になったのか
かゆいのは許せなかったのか
偽善の私がそうさせたのか

あぁ　最後のもがきが聞こえる
あぁ　きっと私を恨んで死んでいったのだろう
１９９４．１０．３

The Sob Which Reverberates through A Wooden Floor

Ah! What a cruel thing I did!
Ah! What a foolish thing I did!
Although I've just decided to be a vegetarian
For a while,
In order to approach Kenji's heart.
Ah, a mosquito is crying,
Ah, he is sobbing reproachfully.
I should have given just a little blood for him
In spite of merely a little itch.
I wonder if I was irritated by the buzz,
I couldn't overlook the itch,
Or my hypocrisy made me do so.
Ah, I can hear the last writhing in discomfort.
Ah, he certainly would have passed away blaming me.

3 October 1994

マカロニサラダ

マカロニサラダのあの頃に戻りたい
秋の風がビュウと吹けば
かすんだオレンジ色の
優しい笑顔が帰って来る
きっと変わらずに風は吹いているのだろう
でも　何かが違う
同じ風に吹かれても
何かが違う
先へ先へと進まなくてはいけないことが
とても悲しい
でも　確かに何かが変わってきているのだ
大空を見上げて
あの頃と変わらないと誓いたいというのに

１９９４．１０．１６

Macaroni Salad

I want to return to the time of macaroni salad.
If the Autumn wind blows,
The tender smiles in misty orange will return.
I believe that the wind has been blowing constantly.
However, something is different.
I feel different.
Even though I'm blown by the same wind.
I'm very unhappy that I have to go
Forward and forward.
But something has certainly been changing.
Although I look up to the great sky and
I want to swear that I'm what I used to be at one time.

16 October 1994

参宮橋のカラス

トコトコ　トコトコ歩いていると
今日は爆弾２つも落とされた
何か私に恨みがあるのかと思ったけれど
きっと人違いをしたのだろう

石を投げる人
矢を引く人
鉄砲を撃つ人
この世の中には怖いものが沢山ある

黒と青紫の体が
近くで　ガァグァ鳴くと怖いけど
それよりも怖いものは沢山あるね
カラスはそれを知っているのだろう

１９９４.１０.１６

A Crow in Sanguubashi

Two bombs were dropped near me today
When I was tottering.
I think that the crow must have mistaken me for someone else
Although I at first thought that
He had ill will towards me.
People who throw stones.
People who shoot arrows.
People who fire guns.
There are a lot of horrible things in this world.
I'm scared of black and bluish-purple crows
When they squawk near me;
However, there are many more brutal things
Than the crows.
They must know it.

16 October 1994

月夜の猫

ネコ　ネコ　何見て　首を傾げる
青い月夜の晩に　何を考えているの

ネコ　ネコ　何見て　笑っているの
半月の空に　ネズミはいるかい

ネコ　ネコ　何をじっと見つめているの
お前の生まれた遠い日を見つめているの

ネコ　ネコ　誰を待っているの
お前のお母さんは何処
何故　首を傾げるの
青い月夜は悲しいね

１９９５.２.７

A MOONLIT NIGHT CAT

Puss, puss,
What are you looking at and
Why are you tilting your head up?
In the blue moonlit night
What are you thinking about?
Puss, puss,
What are you looking at and laughing at?
Is there a mouse in the sky of a
Half moon?
Puss, puss,
What are you gazing at?
Are you gazing at the distant day
When you were born?
Puss, puss,
Who are you waiting for?
Where is your Mother?
Why do you tilt up your head?
A blue moonlit night is sorrowful, isn't it?

7 February 1995

十月のホームは・・・

寒い朝　私はホームで電車を待っている
でも　本当は何を待っているのか
分からない

おおう、人は何故愛するのだろう
この世の中に永遠の愛はないというのに
何故　繰り返し　繰り返し
同じことを繰り返すのか

あの大きな炎のように
燃え上がった愛はどこへ行ったのか
あの誓いはどこへ行ったのか

愛は虚しいだけならば
この電車のように
素早く通り過ぎておくれ
私は失望の目で静かに見送るだろう

1995.2.7

132

The October Platform

On a cold morning
I'm waiting for a train at a platform.
Yet I don't actually know
What I'm waiting for.
Oh, why do people love
Although there is no eternal love
In this world?
Why do people repeat the same thing
Constantly?
Where has the love which flamed out
Like a huge blaze gone?
Where has the oath gone?
If love is just vanity,
Please pass as quickly as this train.
I'll see it off quietly with my disappointed eyes

7 February 1995

イーハトーヴに行った時のこと

鮮やかな光の速さで
緑の涙の大海を渡り
煙が天に昇る中
透明なガラスの階段を駆け上り
真っ白な真珠の玉を集め
七色の孔雀の背に乗り
空を飛んだ

あの素晴らしい日はもう1度来るかな
ねぇ　お父さん

おぼろげに浮かぶ月は
黒鳥をも照らしたよね
ねぇ　お母さん

涙は乾くものだね
ねぇ　お姉さん

1995.2.7

My Memory of when We Went to Ihatoobu

We crossed the mighty green ocean of tears
With the speed of vivid light.
We ran up the transparent glass stairs
While smoke was climbing up into the sky.
We gathered white pearls and
Flew in the sky
On the back of a seven-colour peacock.
Say, Father,
Do you think that the wonderful day will
Come again?
Say, Mother,
The hazy moon illuminated a black swan,
Didn't it?
Say, Sister,
Our tears will dry, won't they?

7 February 1995

ビクトリアスクエア

首を傾げてねだっても
あげる物は何もない
私は貧しい　ただの旅行者
ひなたぼっこを楽しんでいるだけ
それでも見せてくれますか
すずめのダンス

縦に揃えば　太陽眺め
円を描けば　ビクトリアスクエア
光に満ちて影法師も踊る

それではパンくずを差し上げましょう

1995.3.6

VICTORIA SQUARE

I don't have anything to give you
Even though you tilt your head up and beg.
I'm just a poor traveler.
I've just enjoyed the sunshine.
Will you show me a sparrow dance
Despite the fact that I am but a poor traveler?
When you make a vertical line,
The sun looks at you.
When you draw a circle,
It looks like Victoria Square.
The shadows also dance together
In the full light.
Then, I'll give you bread crumbs.

6 March 1995

The Sky of Newzealand

大嫌いだったこの空も
今は離れることがとても悲しい

先日　空を見ました
こんなに大きな空があったんだナと思いました
この空をもう見られないと 考えた時
悲しかったですね
今　私が見ているこの空は
きっと　後で日本で見られるでしょう
でも　同じ空ではありません
あぁ　せめて
もう少しいられたらなと思うばかりです
私はいつの間にか
この空が好きになっていたのです

１９９５．３．６

THE SKY OF NEW ZEALAND

It's a pity now that I have to leave
This sky which I didn't like before.
I looked at the sky the other day.
I realised that there was such a vast sky.
When I thought that I wouldn't be able to
Look at this sky anymore,
I felt so sad.
I will be able to look at the sky which
I'm looking at now in Japan at a later time,
But it won't be the same sky.
Oh, I just wish I could stay here
Even a little longer.
I took to this sky before I knew it.

6 March 1995

椅子

静かに音楽は流れ
ひっそりと静まった部屋は
まるで最後の夜のようだ

この椅子も　この席も
すっかり私に馴染んでいるのに
もうお別れしなければならないなんて
残念も残念だ

せめてこの曲が終わるまで
居て良いと言うならば
私はずっとかけているだろう
このステレオが壊れるまで
このＣＤが壊れるまでは

それが出来ない代わりに
今　いっぱい目に焼き付けておくとしよう
1995.3.11

A Chair

The music is being played softly and
The room is so quiet, like the last evening.
It's really a shame that
I have to say good bye so soon,
Although I completely adjusted to
To this chair.
I'll be sitting here for a while longer
If you tell me that I may stay
At least until the music finishes.
Until this stereo breaks.
Until this CD breaks.
I'll print this scene on my memory
As much as is possible now
Instead of staying longer, which I cannot.

11 March 1995

天女の都

ここは北国　福島かしら？

いいえ　そうではありません

では何故雪が沢山あるの？

あれは雪ではありません

あんなに大地に広がっているのに？

大地はもっと下に広がっています

では、ここは何処なのですか？

ここは天の都です

天女がそこで唄っているではありませんか

１９９５.３.１３

CELESTIAL NYMPH'S CITY

I wonder if this is northern Japan,
Fukushima.
No, it isn't.
Then why is there so much snow?
That isn't snow.
But it is spread so widely upon the Earth?
The Earth spreads far below.
Then where is this place?
This is a celestial city.
A celestial nymph is singing there,
Isn't she?

13 March 1995

親切なＳｅａ　ｇｕｌｌさん

授業をサボった午後
日焼けを楽しみながら
昼寝をしていると・・・

コツ　コツ　コツ

誰かしら
私のブーツを叩くのは
あなたは海のＳｅａ　ｇｕｌｌさん
私を呼びに来てくださったのね
クラスメイトの代わりに

　　　　　　　　　　　　１９９５.３.１３

144

A Kind Seagull

One afternoon when I skipped a class,
When I was taking a nap
Enjoying getting a suntan....
Kotsu, Kotsu, Kotsu,
Who is rapping upon my boots?
You are Mr. Seagull from the sea.
You called to me
Instead of my classmates.

13 March 1995

ドナドナ気分

あの日　彼らはずっと見送ってくれました
軍人さんのように、揃って敬礼をしてくれました
私は手動の扉の中で
胸がいっぱいになりました
夕日に照らされて
ドナドナの気分でした
彼らが見えなくなった時
泣いてしまいました
夕日が目に沁みるとは
こんな感じなのかしらと思いました

１９９５.３.１４

FEELING AS *DONA DONA*

One day they saw me off.
As if they were soldiers they
Saluted me together.
I was so impressed by the car which
Had a manual door.
I felt that I was *Dona Dona*
Illuminated by the late afternoon sun.
I cried in spite of myself
When they were too far away for me
To look at.
I wondered if the expression,
Yuuhi ga me ni shimiru*
Means a situation like this one.

14 March 1995

*The late afternoon sunlight stings my eyes

夏が来ると・・・

あの人に無性に会いたい
夏が来ると無性に会いたくなる
だから　岩手へ行こう

ゆらら　ゆららと　辺りは揺らめき
田んぼも揺らめき
あの人は　きっと　いるだろう
この道を歩き　あの海岸で
遊んでいるのだろう
あの人は私の青春
そして　そこはイーハトーヴ
時間を止めて
きっと私を待っている

ドリームランドで会いましょう
　　　　　　　　　　1995.8.2

WHEN SUMMER COMES...

I really want to see this person.
When summer arrives
I become so eager to see him
Let's go to Iwate prefecture!
Yurara, Yurara... the vicinity curls up
And the rice fields sway.
I'm sure that he is there.
I think that he is walking on this path
And is playing on the beach.
He was my passion in my youth and
It's Ihatoobu.
He stopped time and
Must be waiting for me there.
Let's meet in dream land!

2 August 1995

泣き虫マリー

小さなマリー
泣き虫マリー
ちんけなヤキモチの眼差しは
捨ててしまえ！！

小さな世界
広がる世界
私もいずれ世界の中に入るだろう
臆病な戸惑う眼差しが現れた

ビク　ビク　ジロ　ジロ
小さなマリー
ビク　ビク　ジロ　ジロ
泣き虫マリー

私　歌を作ったの
子守唄にしてあげるね
それから　英語も
もっと上手になって
教えてあげるね

うーん　マリーは泣き虫だね

１９９５.8.2

150

CRY-BABY, MARIE

Little Marie.
Cry-baby Marie.
Discard those small jealous eyes!
Small world.
Yours will become a wide world.
I'll be part of her world someday.
Timid confused eyes appeared.
Biku biku, jiro jiro
Cry-baby Marie.
I made a song for you.
I'll sing the song as your lullaby.
I'll also become better at English
And teach you.
Well, you are a real cry-baby, aren't you?

2 August 1995

"Little Angel"

You are a little baby
little baby little baby
Please show me your face

You are a cute baby
cute baby cute baby
Please smile for me anytime

You are a little angel
little angel little angel
Please sing an angel song

Happy Birthday
to a little baby
Happy Birthday
to a cute baby
Happy Birthday
to a little angel

Happy Birthday to You

1995.6

LITTLE ANGEL

You are a little baby,
Little baby, little baby,
Please show me your face.
You are a cute baby,
Cute baby, cute baby,
Please smile for me.
You are a little angel,
Little angel, little angel.
Please sing an angel song.
Happy birthday to the little baby.
Happy birthday to the cute baby.
Happy birthday to the little angel.
Happy birthday to you.

June 1995

遠いふるさと

モヘアのかかった空を見つめていると
思い出す　遠いふるさと

あの頃の私は今何をしている
あの頃の夢は何処行った
そよぐ風は知っている
どうか　私に教えておくれ

だけど　風は黙ったまんま
通り過ぎてゆき
映し出す
遠いふるさと

1995.9.23

My Faraway Hometown

When I gaze at the mohair-veil sky,
It reminds me of my faraway hometown.
What is that girl doing now?
Where did the dream of those days go to?
The breathing wind knows it.
Would you tell me the answers?
However, the wind passed me
Keeping the secrets and then
Imaged my faraway hometown for me.

23 September 1995

秋の演奏

虫の音　虫の音　蝉の声

涼しくなったら
虫の音　虫の音　鈴虫の声
リズムに合わせて歌ってる
あの日　ポトリと落ちた蝉は
動かなくなった
蝉に代わって歌っても
いつまで聞かせてくれるのか
秋の淋しい

虫の音　虫の音　鈴虫の音

1995.9.23

AUTUMN PERFORMANCE

Bugs' music, bugs' music, cicadas' songs.
When it became cooler.
Bugs' music, bugs' music,
Bell-ringing crickets' songs.
They are singing time to the rhythm.
A cicada that fell down from a tree
Didn't move anymore that day.
When will you play your music for us until
Even you are playing instead of the cicada?
Autumn sorrowful
Bugs' music, bugs' music,
Bell-ringing crickets' songs.

23 September 1995

蜘蛛

蜘蛛　ごめん
お前は父親を探して来たんだね
昨日　お前の父親は谷へ下りた

蜘蛛　ごめん
小さいお前は　妹　だね
今　お前のお兄さんは谷へ下りた

蜘蛛　ごめん
子供の餌を探していたんだね
谷で一緒になっておくれ
そして
もう　ここへ来てはいけないよ
私も辛いのだ

あぁあ　また白い蜘蛛

１９９５.１０.１

SPIDERS

Spider, I'm sorry.
You came to look for your Father,
Didn't you?
Your Father went down
A gorge yesterday.
Spider, I'm sorry.
Small spider, you are his younger sister,
Aren't you?
Your older brother went down
A gorge just now.
Spider, I'm sorry.
You were looking for food for your children
Weren't you?
Please be together in the gorge and
Don't come here anymore.
I also feel terrible.
Ah, a white spider just appeared!

10 January 1995

東京タワーの隣の公園

のどかな午後の公園で
フワフワ綿菓子
雲の木を見つけました
優しい秋の風に吹かれて
雲の木はどんどん育ってゆくのでしょう

そこは小鳥の憩いの場
今日の出来事　話します
夢の話が出た時に
雲の木はもっと大きくなって
東京タワーを追い越したいと言いました

１９９５．１０．２３

A Park next to Tokyo Tower

I found a cloud-tree like soft candy floss
In a peaceful afternoon park.
The cloud-tree will be growing quickly
Being blown by a tender autumn wind.
It is a resting place for birds.
They talk about today's events.
The cloud-tree said that
He wanted to grow up more and
Take over Tokyo Tower
When they were talking about their
Dreams to each other.

23 October 1995

十三夜

十三夜のお月さんが見ているから
恥ずかしい
おなご　おなご　おなごだらけの
ほてった体を
夜風で休め
見せたうなじがより艶っぽい
お月さん　一緒に入ろうよ
箱根のお湯は　えぇ湯ぜよ
と、でも言っているかのように

１９９５．１１．５

162

The Thirteenth Night

I'm embarrassed because
The moon of the thirteenth night is looking at me.
Women, women, only women's
Bodies in its glow are rested by the evening wind,
And the napes of their necks, which they show, are sexy.
As if they are talking like this:
"Hey, the moon!
Let's take a bath together!
A hot spring in Hakone is good!"

5 November 1995

炭酸水

透明な炭酸水は小さな宇宙
何処からともなく
沢山の生命の泡が誕生して
だんだん大きく
だんだん大きく
そして　すぅーと早く飛んでゆく
すぅーと早く死んでゆく
また無数の泡が生まれては
小さな宇宙の中を飛んでゆく
何処へゆくのか　知りたいけど
それを知ることは出来ないの

1995.11.5

164

SODA WATER

Transparent soda water is
A small universe.
Many lives of bubbles are born
From somewhere.
They are getting bigger little by little.
They are getting bigger little by little.
And they fly quickly, smoothly.
They pass away quickly, smoothly.
Countless bubbles are born again, and
They fly in the small universe.
I can't know it,
Although I want to know
Where they are going to.

5 November 1995

満員電車

押しくらまんじゅう　押されて泣くな
押しくらまんじゅう　押されて泣くな
寒い時には
押しくらまんじゅうをすれば良いことを
大人は知っている

でも　みんな　顔が
怒っている　怒っている
鬼のように　怒ってる
みんな　あの日に　戻りたいと思っているに
違いない

押しくらまんじゅう　押されて泣くな
押しくらまんじゅう　押されて泣くな
子供の時の押しくらまんじゅう
大人になった時の為の練習だったの

でも　みんな
違ってる　違ってる
心の中が　違ってる
みんな　あの時は何を思って
押しくらまんじゅうしていたのだろう

1996.1.12

166

FULL TRAINS

Oshikura Manjuu,
Don't cry when you are pushed!
Oshikura Manjuu,
Don't cry when you are pushed!
Adults know that it's good to play
Oshikura Manjuu when we feel cold.
Yet their faces show
Their anger, anger.
They look furious.
I believe that they all must be hoping to
Return to the time.
Oshikura Manjuu,
Don't cry when you are pushed!
Was Oshikura Manjuu in the cradle
A practice in order to adopt to
A rush hour train when we grew up?
Yet they all are different, different.
Their hearts are different from
What they once were.
What were they thinking about
While they were playing Oshikura Manjuu?

12 January1996

引越しの朝

狭い部屋
本当に狭い部屋だな

ダンボールを座布団に
チップスをポリポリかじれば
空間全てに響き渡る
お隣さんに聞こえはしないか
最後にして初めて気を使う

親しい人とのお別れは
淋しいけれど
今　そんな感じかな

ご機嫌よう
さようなら

1996.1.30

MORNING OF MOVING

A narrow room.
It's a really narrow room.
When I nibbled crisps on a flat cushion
That was made from a cardboard box,
The sound echoed throughout the room.
At last, for the first time,
I was concerned whether our neighbours would hear it or not.
We feel sad
When it's a farewell to people who are close to us.
Now I have a similar feeling.
Cheerio!
So long!

30 January 1996

本当に最後の日

本当に最後の日
あなたは見送りに
わざわざ　私のために
出て来て下さったのですね
どうもありがとう

そして　今まで　どうもありがとう
突然出て来て驚かされたあの日のこと
私は忘れます
ですから　あなたも
私が谷へ突き落としたこと
水に流して下さいね

　妹さんやお父さんは
お元気ですか

新しい住人が来たら
あなたは　また姿を現すのでしょう
きっと　私のようにびっくりしますよ
殺されないように気を付けて

　ご機嫌よう

１９９６.１.３１

The Really Last Day

On the really last day
You came out and took out the time
To see me off, didn't you?
Thanks very much!
Thank you for everything!
I'll forget about the incident which
Surprised me so much, when you appeared
Suddenly on that day.
So would you also forgive me
For having pushed you down to the gorge?
How is your younger sister? And your Father?
If new residents come here,
You will show up again, won't you?
They must be as surprised to see you as I was.
Be careful not to be killed!
Cheerio!

31 January 1996

桜新町の蜘蛛に挨拶を

おやっ！！　何故　あなたがここに？
まさか　私の後を追って？
でも　ちょっと違うみたい
蜘蛛は何も言わないけれど
走り去るその姿を見たら
私には分かった

参宮橋の蜘蛛は元気かな
参宮橋は春がよく似合っていたな
もうすぐ　その季節だったのにな

ぼんやり思えば　何かの視線
はっ　もう引越ししたのだ
ここにいる蜘蛛に悪いかな

宜しくね
もう一つの心はそう思っているんだよ
　　　　　　　　　　　　　　１９９６.２.１０

172

A Greeting to a Spider in Sakura Shin Machi

Dear! Why are you here?
Don't say you followed me.
But this spider looks a little different.
This spider didn't say anything,
However, I understood
When I saw that he ran.
I wonder if the spider in Sanguubashi
Is fine.
I remember Sanguubashi goes with spring.
The season would nearly come, though.
When I was thinking so idly,
I noticed someone's gaze.
I gasped. I've already moved here.
I may be rude to the spider here.
Nice to meet you!
I'm thinking so in another part of my mind.

10 February 1996

片思い

片思いって　何て馬鹿馬鹿しくって
くだらなくって
人を不愉快にさせるものなんだ
私は二度と片思いなんてしないぞ

何故　私が　ドキドキ　ワクワク
そして　時にはがっくり、、、なんてことに
ならなくちゃいけないわけ！？
実に不愉快極まりない

この世から　片思いなんて
消え去れ！

1996.2.10

174

Unrequited Love

How ridiculous, silly, and obnoxious
Unrequited love is!
I'll never accept unrequited love again!
Why does my heart have to throb
And at last be sometimes disappointed!?
It's really annoying indeed.
Disappear unrequited love
From this world!

10 February 1996

阿武隈川　白鳥の里

このほとりは　夏の海水浴場
陸地で　少ないお日様
日焼けを楽しむ
金管楽器とカスタネットの大演奏
陽気に自由に奏でてる
向こうで水中逆立ち　楽しむカモは
仲良くなった白鳥と
今度はシベリアへ行こうと
考えているのかな

1996.2.13

176

ABUKUMA-GAWA: VILLAGE OF SWANS

This riverside is a summer swimming place.
They enjoy sun tanning with a little sunshine on the banks.
The great performance of brass instruments and castanets.
They are playing merrily, freely.
I wonder if the ducks that enjoy
Standing on their heads underwater
Over there are thinking of going to
Siberia with the swans that
They have already become friends with.

13 February 1996

私

私というものは
自見良津枝という人間の体を借りて
生きている
だから　自見良津枝が疲れた時は
励ましてあげる

自見良津枝
頑張れ　頑張れ
私も頑張るから　もうちょっとだけ
頑張れ

自見良津枝が傷ついた時は
とても　悲しくなってしまう
可哀想な自見良津枝と
時々泣いてしまう

そして
傷つけたものは許さない
私はどんな時でも私についてきてくれる
自見良津枝がとても大好きだ
だから　とても大切で
誰よりも愛しく可愛がってしまうのだ

1996.3.12

MYSELF

I'm living, but borrowing the body of
A human whose name is Mitsue Jimi.
So I encourage her when she's tired.
Mitsue Jimi,
Cheer up, cheer up!
Keep doing your best a little more
As I'll also do my best!
When she is hurting, I become very sad.
I sometimes cry for poor Mitsue Jimi
And will never forgive anyone who hurts her.
I really love she who follows me whatever happens.
Therefore, she is the most important
And adorable person to me.
That's why I cherish her so much.

12 March 1996

あの人

あぁ　もし　あの人が死んだら
私は狂人になってしまうだろう
言葉も光も失って
あの人の声が再び聞こえるのを
待つだけ
私の目や耳や　どれでも
変わりに授けるから
どうか　あの人だけは
死なせないで
それが出来ぬのなら
いっそ　私も殺して欲しい
と　願う気持ち

　　　　　　　　　１９９６.３.１２

THE PERSON

Oh, I would go crazy
If that person died.
I would lose my voice and light,
And I would just wait to hear that person's voice,
Until I could hear it again.
Please don't let that person die.
I'll give you my eyes, ears, and anything else
Instead!
If it's impossible,
Better yet, I hope that you would kill me
As well.

12 March 1996

春って素敵な季節だから

ルルル　ルルル・・・
風が囁くの
もうすぐ春だよって歌いながら
まだ見えない草花の芽も
こっそり話し掛けてる
私には分かる
春の訪れが
だって　みんなが教えてくれるもの
ルルル　ルルル・・・
歌いながら
桜新町　初めての春
きっと　素敵なことでしょう

１９９６.３.１４

BECAUSE SPRING IS A WONDERFUL SEASON

Ru, ru, ru... Ru, ru, ru....
The wind whispers that
Spring is coming soon
Singing a song.
Buds of plants, which we can't see yet,
Also talk to us secretly.
I can know the arrival of spring
Because they all tell me that,
Singing a song:
Ru, ru, ru... Ru, ru, ru....
The first spring in Sakurashinmachi.
I'm sure that it'll be fantastic.

14 March 1996

四月雨

駅の軒下にしたたる　この雨は
五月雨よりも　ひと月早い
しとやかな雨
心の入れ替えをスムーズにさせる
リラクゼーション
来年も　再来年も　この雨にあったら
きっと　同じことを思うのでしょう
この中では　電車に乗っても
時間はゆっくりと進むのです

1996.4

April Rain

The rain, which drips under the eaves
Of the station, is a graceful rain
That comes one month earlier than
The May rain.
It is relaxing and
Refreshes us smoothly.
Probably I'll have the same feelings
If I meet this rain next year,
And the following year as well.
Time passes slowly in this rain,
Even though we are on a train.

April 1996

太陽

太陽の光ってすごいよ
眩し過ぎて　目を開けてられない
電車で逃げても　逃げても
追いかけてくるんだ
やる気をいっぱい出してくれる
うん、生きようって　強く思うんだ
ショボン・・・と、してても
こんなに照らされちゃ
笑うしかないね
だから　ちょっと照れ笑いで
変な顔になっちゃったよ

１９９６.４.１２

THE SUN

Sunlight is amazing.
I can't keep my eyes open
Because it's so bright.
Even though I run away, on and on
On a train,
It chases after me.
It makes me very energetic
With a strong will to live.
I was depressed
But I had no choice except to smile
Because I was brightly illumined
By the sunlight.
So, I smiled bashfully a little
With a funny look on my face.

12 April 1996

たんぽぽ　－動物園へ行く途中－

いつでも会える
何処でも会える
そう思っていたので
特別　気にしていませんでしたが
久し振りに会ってみると
最後に会ったのは
遥か彼方遠く
　私の幼い思い出と共に
ゆるやかな風に揺られ
よみがえる野原
たんぽぽ　ぺんぺん草　バラなどなど

あの小さな白い花は何というのだろうか
　　　　　　　　　１９９６.５.４

Dandelions

(on my way to the zoo)

I hadn't paid special attention to them
Because I had thought that
I would be able to see them anytime, anywhere.
However, when I at last saw them,
After a while,
I realised that a very long time had passed
Since we last met.
It's in the field to which I return
In my memories of childhood,
Swayed by a gentle breeze.
Dandelions, Shepherd's-purses, roses....
I wonder what the name of
Those small white flowers is.

4 May 1996

肉体と精神

この肉体と精神は別なものである
肉体は私によくついてきてくれる

私はかつて私自身を欠陥人間だと思っていた
背は低く　髪の毛も繭も薄く
額は横幅がなく
目の大きさも　鼻の穴の大きさも左右違い
頬は赤く　歯並びも悪く
首は長く　左手の人差し指の爪は曲がり
お尻は大きく　足の親指はテレビで
声は低い　目も悪い
一体　こんな私を
どうしたら好きになれるだろうか

しかし　後々好きになった
一生懸命ついてきてくれる　この肉体を
愛しく思えるようになったのである

ところが　新たな嫌悪感が私の中に
生まれ出てきている
あの頃思った欠陥なんかは欠陥ではなかった
私を欠陥人間ならしめているものは
肉体ではなく　この精神である
今の私は父や母や家族から与えられた
大切なものを失いつつあるのだ

年を取るごとに　それは失われていき
私は何とも貧しい人間となってしまった

ある時は　意識の中にありつつも　ないようにし
また　ある時は
無意識のうちに邪悪なものが飛び出す
私は笑っていても笑っていない
いずれ　この精神は分裂を始め

私は私ではなく
別の者が支配するのかもしれない
いつでも二つの思想が浮かぶ世界は
後に天と地をも　真っ二つに分け
どうにかなってしまうのだろう
私の中に住む　私の知らない
この邪悪な怪物は
私の大切なものを減少させ
私は再び欠陥人間になってしまった

子供の頃に戻りたいと強く願うのは
そのためかもしれない

　　　　　　　　　１９９６.５.５

Body and Spirit

This body and its spirit are different.
My body always follows me.
I used to feel myself a faulty man.
I'm short.
My hair and eyebrows are thin.
My forehead is narrow.
There are differences in the size of my left and right
Eyes and nostrils.
My cheeks are red.
My teeth are crooked.
My neck is long.
My left index fingernail is crooked.
My big toes look like a television.
My hips are large.
My voice is too low.
I have poor eyesight.
How can I like such a one as myself?
But I warmed to myself later.
I came to love this body
Which follows me no matter what happens.
However, a new abhorrence has appeared
In my mind.
The defects I saw those days were not
Real defects.
What makes me a faulty man is not
This body, but this spirit.
Recently I've been losing an important
Thing that was given to me by my parents:
My family.
The older I get, the more I lose it.
I became a poor man.
One time
I pretend that I don't have,

Even though I know that I do have.
Another time
The dark spirit came out without my intending it to.
I don't really smile even though I appear to.
Someday this spirit may leave
And another might dominate me.
I may not be me in the future.
I think the world in which
Two thoughts always exist will divide
Even heaven and earth
In two, and they will become something crazy.
As the unknown vicious monster
Which lives inside me made
The important thing in me decrease,
I became a faulty man again.
It may be because of this
That I really wish to return to
My childhood.

5 May 1996

他人と自分

私は自分をとても可愛がっている
だから　疲れていたりすると
可哀想に思う

だけど　人はそうじゃない
あまり親身になってくれない人もいる
そんな時　とてもがっかりして
もう１人　自分がいればいいのになって思う
あぁ　この人も自分のことだけ
考えているのだわ　と思う

私がもう１人いれば
私のこと　本当に可愛がって
私のこと　本当に思ってくれるのに

1996.6.3

OTHERS AND ME

I really cherish myself,
So I feel pity for me
When I'm tired.
But others are not like me.
There are people who don't care for me.
Then I'm very disappointed and
Think I would be very happy
If another Mitsue Jimi existed.
Oh, I feel this person is also
Thinking only about oneself.
If another me existed,
She would really cherish me and
Consider me very much, though.

3 June 1996

黒い喋喋

必死に勉強して
必死にテストを受ける私達を
あざ笑う　黒い喋喋

もうスピードで通路を駆ける試験官の勢いに
吹き飛ばされる　黒い喋喋

余裕のない人間達の足で
踏み潰されそうになる　黒い喋喋

テストが開始されれば
私にも
お前のことを考える余地はない

五日経って　今　やっと思い出したのだ
　　　　　　　　　１９９６.6.13

A Black Butterfly

It's a black butterfly that cynically
Laughs at we who are taking exams
Desperately after studying so hard.
It's a black butterfly that is blown by
A supervisor who runs with high speed
Through an aisle.
It's a black butterfly that is nearly stepped on by
The feet of humans who don't make room
For other things.
I also don't have space in my head
To think about you
Once the exam begins.
After five days had passed, I remembered.

13 June 1996

岩手県のあの人

夏になると　会いたくなる　あの人に
私にとって　人間にとって
大切なものは何なのかを
教えてくれる　あの人に

私は一体何をしなければならないのか
何が出来るというのかを
教えてくれる　あの人に

目まぐるしい日常を脱して
異次元の世界へと導くあの人は
今　ここにいない

それでも　会いたいと思うのは
純粋への憧れが
胸いっぱいに広がった時なのでしょう

１９９６．８．２６

The Person in Iwate Prefecture

When summer comes,
I'll be eager to see the person who
Teaches us what things are important
For me, for us.
I will want to see the person who
Can teach me what I should do and
What I can do.
The person who leads me to
The world of different dimensions,
Which does not require me to lead a hurried daily life,
Is not here now.
It will be when my heart is full of
Longing for innocence
That I would like to see him,
Even though I know
He is not here now.

26 August 1996

蟬

ミーン　ミーン
儚い夏の声

たったの　ほんのわずかな命
一体　誰が定めたの
心は何を思っているの
花は来年もまた咲くけれど
その声を聞くことは出来ないね
そういうのを運命というの
明日　私はどうなるか分からない
でも　花も私も希望はあるのに
夏の声は儚い

ミーン　ミーン
儚い

ミーン　ミーン
儚い

１９９６.８.２６

CICADAS

Miin, miin.
Short-lived voice in summer.
A mere tiny life.
Who on earth decided it?
What are they feeling in their hearts?
Though flowers boom next year again,
And I can see it,
I can't hear the voice again.
Should I call it fate?
I don't know what will happen to me tomorrow,
But there is hope both for me and for flowers.
The summer voice is frail.
Minn, minn.
It's fragile.
Minn, minn.
It's fragile.

26 August 1996

２２日の夜

台風が去った後の空は
純粋な夜空
東京で初めて見る　綺麗な星空
強い風が　一切を
吹き飛ばしたのだろう
東京での私の心は
スモッグがかかった空

台風よ　来い
もう一度　綺麗な星を見せておくれ

１９９６.９.２６

THE NIGHT OF THE TWENTY-SECOND

The sky after a typhoon is a clear night sky.
It is a beautiful starry sky in Tokyo such as
I have never seen before.
It seems that a strong wind cleared everything.
My heart in Tokyo is like a smog-filled sky.
Come on, typhoon!
Please show me the beautiful stars
Again.

26 September 1996

ピクニックランド回想

便秘の時に便を出すのは一苦労だが
母体が生命を誕生させるのはもっと大変

あぁ　またそんなことを考えて
今日は折角の月一の楽しみだというのに
素敵な野や山
広大な自然の中で
おいしい肉や野菜を沢山ほおばれる
この瞬間は幸せであるはずなのに

ドクン　ドクン

心臓が鳴って暗い気持ちになるのは何故だろう
今だけ辺りが何も見えない程
真っ暗になってくれればいいのに

そんな溜息をつく私を
さっき会ったばかりの
ホルスタイン
チョコレート
ポップコーン
太郎らは何と思いながら
眺めているのだろうか

                    １９９６．１０．１４

204

Reminiscence of Picnic Land

It's hard to go to the toilet
When we are constipated.
But it's much harder to give birth to a baby.
Oh, I'm thinking about such a thing again,
Although today is my precious day to have fun,
Once a month.
Though I should be happy at this moment,
When I can eat a lot of delicious
Meat and vegetables,
In the midst of extensive Nature,
Wonderful fields and mountains.
Dokun, dokun,
Why is my heart beating and
Why am I so gloomy?
I wish it could be so dark that
We couldn't see anything around here only now.
I wonder what they are thinking about me
Who am sighing and suffering
While they are looking at me,
Who they just now met.
Holstein,
Chocolate,
Popcorn,
Tarou.

14 October 1996

１９９６ 秋 初みかん

すっぱいみかんは遠足の味
絵の具で書いたみたいな紅葉眺めて
おべんと食べた
小さい紅葉みたいな手いっぱいに
松ぼっくり拾った
あの頃長く感じた出来事も
今となってはほんの一瞬
すっぱいみかんの思い出
よみがえる思い出

１９９６.１０.１６

206

The First Mandarin Orange of Autumn 1996

Sour mandarins taste like
The mandarin, which I ate on a school trip.
I ate my lunch while viewing multi-coloured leaves
Which looked like a watercolour painting.
My hands looked like small maple leaves.
I picked up many pine cones until my hands were full.
This event, which seemed to last for a long time in those days,
Seems like just a moment to me now.
My memory of the sour mandarin.
It is a memory that revives me.

16 October 1996

富士山

おっきいね
富士山はおっきいね
どんなことが巻き起ころうとも
ビクともしない
どんと構えて立っている
ひどい嵐がやってきても
春風がふんわり吹き抜けたように
笑っている
私もそんなふうになりたいな
おっきく　おっきくなれるかな
富士山よりも大きくね

1996.10.22

208

Mt. Fuji

It's big, isn't it?
Mount Fuji is very big, isn't it?
It's standing steadily without shaking
No matter what has happened.
Even if a horrible storm comes,
Mt. Fuji smiles,
As if it is merely a spring wind, skimming across the land mildly.
I want to be like Mt. Fuji,
Am I able to become big?
I want to be bigger than Mt. Fuji.

22 October 1996

無題

まだ幼く小さい頃に
戻りたいと思うことがありますか
私は強く強くそれを願うのです

絶対叶うことのないことと知りながら
タイムマシーンでもなければ
戻ることなんて出来ないと分かっていても
もう　あの時代の　あの場所の
あの家族はないと知りながら
今がどんなに幸せであっても
あの頃を思えば
どんな楽しいことも　成功も
ちっぽけなものに見えてしまうのです

あの平和で幸福であったあの頃を思えば
いいえ　決して平和でもなく
幸福であったともいえないかもしれない
なのに　あの頃と同じような風が吹く度
空がゴォーと音をたてる度
私の記憶はあの頃に戻り
強く強く幼少の頃に戻りたいと願うのです

しかし　もし神様が私の願いを叶えて下さって
戻れたとしても　ただ戻っただけならば
同じことを繰り返し　大人になった私は

再び同じことを願うことになるでしょう

今の脳みそを持って戻ったとしても

あの頃とは違い

別の歴史を歩むことになるでしょう

今の私のこの願いは

全ての結果が出た後に思うことであり

もっと最悪の結果を招くことにもなりかねません

風に吹かれる度

空の音を聞きながら

私は絶対叶うことのない願いを

繰り返し　繰り返し　考え

それが私の人生というのならば

何と儚く薄暗い人生であるといえましょう

私に感情というものがある限り

私はこの願いを永遠に抱き続け

自分の一生を終えるのではないかと思います

１９９７.１.７

UNTITLED

Do you sometimes think that
You would like to return to your childhood?
I really really hope to return,
Although I know that dream will never come true.

Unless we have a time machine or something,
It's impossible to return.
I also know that the family I knew
At that place, in those days,
Doesn't exist anymore.
Yet, any joy and success that I have these days seem to be
But tiny things,
No matter how happy I am now
When I remember that moment,
When I think of those days when
I was in that peaceful and happy world.

No, I might not be able to say that
It was entirely peaceful and happy,
But my memories of those times returns, and
I wish to return to my childhood with all my might
Each time I feel that same wind
Blowing as before,
Each time I hear the sound
The sky makes.

However, I would repeat the same
Things again as I grow older and
End up wishing for the same things again,
If I just returned to my childhood,
Thanks be to God.
Even if I returned to my childhood as
I am now,
It would be different,
And would happen differently.
It would lead to a worse outcome.
This current wish of mine is the wish
I made after all the consequences of past actions
Had happened and gone.

Each time the wind blows on me,
I hear the sound of the sky and
Repeatedly wish the same wish
Which will never come true.
If this is to be my life,
I will say that life is fragile and dim.
I think that I will hold onto this wish forever
Until I finish my life,
As long as I have emotions.

7 January 1997

11月のある朝のこと

11月のある朝のこと
開店前のお店の扉の前に
一匹の猫がおりました
猫は
開けてぇー　開けてぇー
と白い息をはきながら言っています
すると　扉の向こうから
人が来る気配
そして　ガチャガチャと
カギを開ける音がしました
「あら、あんた。また朝帰りなの？」
その声の主はネグリジェに
スリッパを履いておりました

11月のある朝のこと
猫は開店前のお店の入り口に
ちょこんと座っておりました
入り口はシャッターが
閉められています
猫は　開けてぇー
と言いませんでした
そのしっぽは
しょぼんとしていました

1997.1.26

214

An Event one November Morning

An Event one November morning.
There was a cat in front of the door of
A shop before opening time.
The cat said with its white breath,
"Open the door. Open the door please."
Then someone seemed to come from
Inside the shop.
The lock turned.
"Well you came back home in the morning again?"
The person who spoke was wearing
A negligee and a pair of slippers.
An Event on another November morning.
The cat was sitting quietly
In front of the entrance of the shop
Before opening time.
The shutter was closed.
"Open the door please," the cat didn't say.
Its tail looked disappointed.

26 January 1997

ごめんね

ごめんなさいね
私　余裕がないの
ごめんなさいね
余裕がないの
ごめんなさいね
今　時間がないの
ごめんなさいね
今　お金がないの
ごめんなさいね
私　心の余裕がないの
ごめんなさいね
自分のことで手一杯
ごめんなさいね
笑顔の余裕がないの
ごめんなさいね
心の余裕がないの
ごめんなさいね
分かってね
分かってね
ごめんなさい

　　　　　　　1997.1.26

216

I'm Sorry

I'm sorry.
I don't have time.
I'm sorry.
No time.
I'm sorry.
I'm too busy.
I'm sorry.
I really can't afford it.
I'm sorry.
I don't have room for any other things in my thoughts.
I'm sorry.
I'm full of thoughts for myself.
I'm sorry.
I don't have space in my heart to smile.
I'm sorry.
I don't have room for you in my mind.
I'm sorry.
Please understand, please understand!
I'm so sorry.

26 January 1997

かざぐるま

倒れた自転車はかざぐるま
夜が来るのは遅くなって
朝が来るのは早くなって
ほのかな春の香りの風が
かざぐるまを回す

いいや　騙されんぞ
昨夜は粉雪が舞っていた
ほら　吐く息もこんなに白い

それでも　もうすぐ春が
訪れる予感がするのです

1997.2.19

PINWHEELS

Bicycles that have fallen over look like pinwheels.
Night falls late and morning visits early.
The wind, which smells faintly of spring
Spins the pinwheels.
No, I won't be deceived!
A fine snow was dancing last night.
Look, my breath is also white.
In spite of those things,
I foresee that spring is coming soon.

19 February 1997

私は主観主義者

私は主観主義者
好きなものは好き
嫌いなものは嫌い
好きな人は好き
嫌いな人は無条件に嫌い

もし　好きな人が
誰かを好きになったら
その誰かは嫌い

好きな人は
私に愛情を注いでくれる
でも　好きな人で
愛情をくれない人もいる

なのに　別な人を好きになって
ニコニコしていたら
その別な人は大嫌い
その愛情は
私だけのものだったらいいのに

でも　マリーは別
マリーは許してあげよう

1997.3.31

I'M SUBJECTIVE

I'm subjective.
I like what I like.
I dislike what I dislike.
I like people whom I like.
I dislike people whom I dislike
Without reasons.
If the person whom I love loves someone else,
I hate that someone.
Some people whom I love give their love to me,
But those who don't give their love to me also exist,
Even though I love them.
If the person whom I love loves another and happily smiles,
I really hate the another.
I wish their love could be given to me only.
However, Marie is different.
I will forgive you, Marie.

31 March 1997

亀は万年

「カメさん、あなたは何年生きられるのですか?」

「私は300年まで生きられます。でも、本当は
　万年まで生きたいところです。」

「何故ですか?」

「私はずっと生きていたいのです。でも、それは
　無理でしょう?だから、せめて万年まで・・・
　あなたは?」

「私は80年位です。以前は人生50年と言わ
　れていましたが、最近は医学の進歩と科学の発
　達により平均80年位となったようです。」

「へぇ、それは良かったですね。」

「いいえ、良くありませんよ。」

「どうしてですか?」

「私は長く生きたくない。」

「何で、また。」

「年を取るにつれて老化していくでしょう?
　この美と知は確実に失われていきます。」

「では、いくつまで?」

「そうですね。30年から35年でいいです。
　しわくちゃになるでしょ?そんな姿になって
　まで生きたくないのです。」

「私はもともと　しわくちゃですが・・・。」

「・・・・・・。」

「・・・・・・。」

1997.3.31

222

Turtle for Perpetual Years

"How many years can you live, Mr. Turtle?"
"I can live for three hundred years.
But to be honest I want to live for
Ten thousand years."
"Why?"
"To tell the truth, I want to live forever,
However, that's impossible, isn't it?
So, at least for ten thousand years....
How about you?"
"In our case, we can live for about eighty years.
It had been said that our life could last
For fifty years, but it seemed that
The recent average is about eighty years
Because of medical science
And the progress of science in general."
"Really, that's good for you, isn't it?"
"Not at all."
"Why is that?"
"I don't want to live for such a long time."
"Why?"
"We are aging as we get older.
Our beauty and intelligence are certainly
Decreasing little by little."
"Then, how long would you like to live?"
"Let me see. I would prefer to live until
Thirty years of age.
Otherwise we will have lines on our face, won't we?
I don't want to live with an aged lined face...."
"Since I was born, I have had a lot of lines on my face...."
"............."
"............."

31 March 1997

福島の風

ふんわり　そよぐ
福島の風は優しい
温かくって優しく包んでくれる
だから　私は
何も気取らずに　気負わずに
自然のまんま
笑っていられる
離れてみて　ちょっとは
好きになったのかな
福島のこと

1997.5.6

WIND IN FUKUSHIMA

The wind that breathes mildly in Fukushima is tender.
It holds me gently, warmly.
Therefore, I can smile naturally
Without effort or eagerness.
I wonder if I warmed to Fukushima a little
Because I left Fukushima.

6 May 1997

"ちぇっ"

晴天の空の下
石ころ蹴って帰ったんだ
ちょっと　いじけて帰ったんだ
みんなと早めにお別れしたのは
そのためだったんだ

一緒にいれば楽しいけれど
少し経てば　またお別れ
楽しいけれど淋しいね
そしたら　いじけ虫がやって来た

晴天の空の下
ちっとも　清々しくなんかない
空なんか見ない
だって　石ころ蹴って
"ちぇっ"なんだもの

1997.5.6

226

"CHI"

I returned home kicking a small stone
Under the blue sky.
I went back home murmuring a little.
That's why I said "Good-bye"
To them earlier.
We have to leave each other again
After just a few moments together.
Although we enjoy being together,
Although being with them makes me happy,
It also makes me sad.
And then I became perverse.
Now the blue sky didn't refresh me at all.
Now I don't look up to the sky
Because my feeling is "Chi"
Kicking the stone.

6 May 1997

悲しいことがあっても

英語　好き
生き甲斐があって良かったナ

私のことを愛してくれる家族がいて
本当に良かったナ

お手紙　どうもありがとう
変わらない友情って　いいものだナって

GTO見て　笑えるのって
本当に幸せだナ

悲しいことがあっても生きていられる
うん　また頑張ろうって思えることは
私は幸せなんだ

うん　また頑張ろうね
自見　良津枝ちゃん

1997.6.8

Even Though Sad Things
Happened

I like English.
I am lucky because I can thrive on this.
I am really lucky, as there is my family who
Love me as I love them.
Thank you for your letter.
Our friendship, which has not changed, is very nice.
I am so lucky that I can laugh
While I am reading GTO.
Even though sad things have happened,
I am still alive.
Yes, I am lucky because I can believe that
I will do my best again.
Yes, let's start doing our best again,
Ms. Mitsue Jimi.

8 June 1997

ゴキブリ

蜘蛛様は天国へ召され
ゴキは地獄へ落ちろ
蜘蛛様は絶対殺せない
逃がしてあげなきゃ
ゴキは早く死んでくれ
この世から消えてくれ
蜘蛛様は天国へ召され
ゴキは地獄へ落ちろ

これでいいのか？
自見　良津枝

１９９７.６.８

COCKROACHES

I hope that spiders go to Heaven
And cockroaches go to Hell.
I can never kill spiders and
Have to let them escape.
Cockroach, please die immediately
And vanish from this world!
I hope that spiders go to Heaven
And cockroaches fall into Hell.
Is this a correct attitude, Mitsue Jimi?

8 June 1997

神様への手紙

神様　私を助けて下さい

私は狂人になりたくないのです
私には愛する家族や
やりたいことも沢山あります
私は心臓発作なんて起こしたくないのです
いつでも健康で楽しく
生きていたいのです

私に力を下さい
私が最後まで頑張れるように

私に力を下さい
私　頑張りますから

1997.7.24

232

A LETTER TO GOD

God, please help me!
I don't want to be crazy.
I have my beloved family and
Many things I want to do.
I don't want to have a heart attack.
I want to live happily, healthily everyday.
Please give me the power,
Please give me the energy to be able to
Do my best until the end.
I will make a strong effort.

24 July 1997

Ｌｕｃｋｙが家にやって来た

命を預かること
幸せな人生を保障すること

責任が重過ぎる
実に責任が重過ぎる
今まで適当に　自由に
好きにやってきた私にとって
これほど　選択するのに
頭を悩ませたことはない

大人になるチャンスかもしれない
これも何かの縁だ
折角　６５のＤになったのだから
心身共に大人にならなければならない

１９９７．８．２７

Lucky Came to our House

To take care of someone's life,
To secure someone's happiness in their life,
These are responsibilities that are too heavy
Indeed for me.
I was never troubled whether to choose yes or no.
Like this time
Because I had lived as I liked,
Irresponsibly, freely.
It might be a chance to be an adult.
It's also something like a strange coincidence.
I have to be an adult mentally and physically,
Because my bust became a 65D.

27 August 1997

デジモンちゃんは逝ってしまった

Ｌｕｃｋｙが優しい秋の風に
顔を撫でられて寝息をたてたあの日
お前は死んでしまったね

２０日ばかりの穏やかな日々は
輝く金粉のようになって
空へ飛んで行った

ほら　ごらん
ほうき星になって空を駆け巡っているよ
こんな胸の締め付けられる出発は
もう　いらない

さようなら　さようなら
ごめんなさいとだけ言うよ

　　　　　　　　　　　　１９９７.９.４

Degimon-chan has Passed Away

On the day when Lucky was sleeping with
Regular breathing,
While his face was being stroked by a
Gentle autumn wind,
Degimon, you died.
The only peaceful twenty days flew into the sky
After they became like brilliant golden powder.
Hey, look!
It turned out to be a comet and is flying
Around in the sky.
I don't want a departure in which
I will be deeply distressed anymore.
Goodbye, farewell!
I will say to him only "I'm sorry."

4 September 1997

どうして嫌われるのかな

どうして　蜘蛛は嫌われるのかな
どうして　豚は笑われるのかな
どうして二十日鼠は殺されるのかな
どうして　あの動物達は食べられちゃうのかな

どうして　どうして

決して　自分達が望んでその姿に
生まれたわけじゃないのにね

１９９７.１０.１４

Why are They Disliked?

Why are spiders disliked?
Why are pigs laughed at?
Why are rats killed?
Why are animals eaten?
Why? Why?
They were not born in those forms
As a result of their own wishes.

                                        14 October 1997

東京

東京
大都会でもなく
憧れの場所でもなく
遊びの場でもない
第二の故郷

あんなに嫌がっていた福島が
無性に恋しくなって
帰る日が近づくと
胸が高鳴るのは
古里だから

東京を離れる時間が
近づくにつれ
何か不安のような
後ろ髪引かれるような
ちょっと　しんみりする気持ちに
なっていったのは
第二の故郷だから

今日　初めて分かった

1997.11.1

240

Tokyo

Tokyo...
It's not a big city or
A cool place for amusement.
It's my second hometown
Since Fukushima is my hometown
I now miss it very much, even though I used to hate it.
And I'm getting excited as the date to return is near.
It's because Tokyo is my second hometown
That I feel anxious, reluctant and
A little bit sad
As the time to leave Tokyo is near.
I recognized that today for the first time.

1 November 1997

三日月

真っ黒の空に
のどかに煌々と浮かぶ三日月
それは冬の田舎の象徴だ
でも　もう後一時間半もすると
もっと　取って付けたような
貧弱な都会の三日月に変化する

同じ月でも全く違うように見えるのは
見る場所が違うからなのか
私の精神状態が違うからなのか

また　当分の間
月を見る余裕すらなくなってしまうのか
それでも　私の胸の中に
今日　見た美しい三日月の記憶をとどめておいて
辛い時に思い出すことにしよう

１９９７.１１.４

242

A Crescent

It's a crescent moon, which rises pastorally,
Brightly in the black sky.
It's a symbol of the winter countryside.
Yet, after one hour and a half
It will change into a poor, urban crescent moon,
Like an artificial one.
I feel it is a different moon
Even though I am looking at the same moon.
Does it depend on the vantage point from which I observe it?
Or does it depend on my mental state?
I wonder if I will be too busy even to look
At the moon for a while again.
However, I will keep my memory of
This beautiful crescent moon I looked at today
In my heart and remember the moon
When life is hard for me.

4 November 1997

欠けた太陽

あの日　私の体の半分が
欠けてしまった
太陽も月も半分になった
宇宙も　この世界全てが
私が生きている意義みたいなものも

私は　ブクブク　ブクブク
白く濁った海の底へ
沈んで行くけど
片方がないから
もがくことも出来ないの

水中から見える欠けた太陽は
ユラユラ　キラキラ
生命の光を降り注ぐ
あぁ　海の底は静かだな
とか思いながら
不思議と苦しくはない
あれは外国船の残骸かしら
喜びと悲しみは背中合わせ
魚達は私の脇を
知らん顔して泳いでく
私は深く深く沈んで行って考える

もし　再びあの月や太陽を
直接眺めることがあるのなら
自分探しの旅へ出掛けよう
あの光へ向かって
出掛けよう

　　　　　　１９９７．１２．２４

245

The Cracked Sun

One day my body lost a half.
The sun and the moon also became halved.
The universe and this entire world as well.
Things like the meaning of my life as well.

I'm not able to even struggle due to the half I lost,
Although I went under a white cloudy seabed:
Buku buku, buku buku.

The cracked sun, which I can see from under the water,
Pours out the light of life:
Yura yura, kira kira.
Oh, I don't choke somehow,
While I'm thinking that the seabed is silent
Or something.
Is that the wreck of a foreign ship?
Joy and sadness are opposite sides of the same coin.
Some fish are swimming beside me,
Ignoring me.
I go down deeply and think.

If I have the chance to
View that moon and that sun
Directly again,
I will travel to look for myself.
I will start toward that light.

24 December 1997

グァム旅行

光があるから影があり
影があるから光がある

♪ジャンジャガ　ジャンジャガ♪

リズムに乗って
ビューンと天国まで
行っちまったよ
そんな感じサ
グァムって所は
それを何だい
あんた　知らないくせに
何言ってんだよ
光があるから影があって
影があるから光があんだよ
だまってなっ！

どうせなら　住みたいね
天国に
みんなでね

　　　　　　　　　1997.12.24

248

A Trip to Guam

There is light therefore there is shadow;
And there is shadow therefore
There is light.
⊠Janjaga janjaga⊠
We went to heaven quickly with rhythm.
Guam is a place like that.
What's that?
How dare you say such a thing
When you don't know anything!
There is light therefore there is shadow;
And there is shadow therefore
There is light.
Keep your mouth shut!
I want to live there, if possible.
It would be nice if we could live in heaven together.

24 December 1997

Ｌｕｃｋｙの独り言

Ｌｕｃｋｙは言う
人間は我儘だな
折角　ｌｕｃｋｙを叶えてやったのに
叶ったとたん　次から次と
不平をもらす
ため息をもらす
欲望を無限に持ってるんじゃないかしらって
付き合いきれないって

　　　　　　　　　　１９９８.１.１８

250

LUCKY'S MURMUR

Lucky said,
"Humans are selfish.
They complain and sigh constantly
Once their dreams come true,
Even though I gave them luck.
I think humans are endlessly lustful.
I can no longer associate with them."

18 January 1998

1月15日 ―雪の朝―

この舞い落ちる雪の中を
ふわふわと飛び回りたい
　（このホームの壁に頭をぶつけたい）
この雪のように
静かに舞い降りたい
　（線路の上に寝転がりたい）
もし　隣に座ったハゲ頭の男に
急にわき腹を刺されたら
　（痛い！　痛い！　それは痛い！）
私の父や母は悲しむだろう
　（生きねばならない）
静かに地面に溶けてゆく
この雪のように
溶けたい
　（ゆっくりと幸せな気持ちで眠りたい）

1998.1.18

252

The Fifteenth of January-
White Morning

I want to flitter about like butterflies
In the snow that was fluttering down.
"I want to hit my head on the wall of this platform."
I want to float down silently like this snow.
"I want to lie down on the railway."
If I am stabbed in the side by a bald man who
Is sitting next to me,
"Painful, painful, it would be painful!"
My parents would be sad.
"I have to stay alive."
I want to melt as this snow melts into
The ground, quietly.
"I want to sleep happily, carefree."

18 January 1998

デジモン挽歌

節分の豆の数
年の数
おもむろに出した数
１６個
それでも　お前が食べる分には
余ってしまう
不意に襲ったお前の死

生きよう　生きよう

節分の豆
お前の分まで食べて
お前の分まで生きてみせよう

１９９８．２．４

ELEGY FOR DEGIMON

The number of beans for Setsubun.
The number of your age.
There are sixteen beans that I took out
Without intending to.
But they will be too much for you.
It was a sudden death, which took you.
I'll live, I'll live.
I will eat your beans for you on Setsubun and
Try living for you.

4 February 1998

Ｌｕｃｋｙはキュッと言った

Ｌｕｃｋｙはキュッと言った
小さい命　守れなくて　ごめん
お前の幸せを保障してやろうなんて
出来なかったよ
分かっていたことなのに
辛い思いさせて　ごめん

お腹いっぱい　食べさせてあげたかったな
お腹いっぱい　向日葵の種
食べさせてあげたかったな
うんと　うんと広い大地で
花と一緒に
回る落ち葉と一緒に
遊ばせてあげたかったな

川も海も雨も知らずに
死んでしまった
澄み切った冬の夜空には
キランと星が光ることも
風がヒュウとなって囁くことも
知らずに
春には薄桃の桜が木にぶら下がって
ユラユラ揺れるんだぞ

なのに　お前は笑って
ほんとに笑って
私に挨拶をしてくれるのかい

１９９８．２．２４
256

Lucky said "Kyu"

Lucky said "Kyu".
I'm sorry I am not able to protect your
Little life.
I wanted to secure your happiness
But I couldn't.
I had known that.
I'm sorry I made you miserable.
I wished I had let you eat as much as you liked.
I wished I had let you eat a lot of
Sunflower seeds.
I hoped that I had let you play with
Flowers and fallen leaves, which danced
Together on the extremely vast field.
You passed away without knowing
Rivers, the sea and rains,
Without knowing that stars shine
In the clear winter night sky and
That winds whisper, making a noise, hyuu.
Do you know that pale pink cherry blossoms
Sway, depending from trees, in spring?
In spite of this,
Will you smile and greet me?

24 February 1998

ある穏やかな日

あの子は春を待たずに
逝ってしまった
春の訪れが何だというのだ

温かく　花の蜜の香りがたちこめる
喜びの季節
幸福の訪れ
それが何だというのだ

私の心は暗く
冷たい冬に閉ざされ
鋭いツララが突き刺さる
悲しき後悔の雪が吹き荒れる
あの子が死んだ今となっては
幸せなど訪れないのだ

通りで会った黒い毛むくじゃらの犬も
私のことを
哀れんで見ていたではないか
春が何だというのだ

１９９８．３．４

A Calm Day

My boy had left before spring arrived.
What is the meaning of the arrival of spring?
It is a season of joy, which is filled with
The scent of warm flower honey.
It is the arrival of happiness.
What does this matter?
My heart is isolated by the dark, cold winter
And stabbed by sharp icicles.
Sad snows of regret are blowing.
Now that my boy died,
Happiness will never again visit me.
A black haired dog that I bumped into
On the street also looked at me with sympathy.
What is the meaning of spring?

4 March 1998

人間とお饅頭

けったり
なぐったり
悪口言ったり
無視したり
そうされても　お饅頭は
悲しまない
悲しさだとか　悔しさだとか
みんな　あんこが吸収するので
いつでも　甘く　おいしく
笑っている

だけど　人間はそうじゃない
悲しかったり　悔しかったり
痛みやショックも
感じるんだよ

人間はお饅頭じゃないんだよ

1998.3.20

HUMANS AND O-MANJUU

Even if it's kicked, punched,
Verbally abused and ignored,
O-manjuu won't be sad.
It's always smiling sweetly, deliciously
Because red beans paste absorbed it all.
However humans are not like O-manjuu.
We feel sad, frustrated, shocked,
And pain.
Humans are not O-manjuu.

20 March 1998

春の訪れ

日毎　暖かくなってきた
春の訪れ
あの猫は　いつの間にか
引越しをしてしまっていた
去年の今頃は
確か　毎朝
表の道路や車の下で
ゴロゴロしていた筈なのに
あのネグリジェは
やっぱり　主人だったのか
Ｌｕｃｋｙもいない
猫もいない
今年の春は淋しいのぅ

１９９８.３.２０

THE ARRIVAL OF SPRING

It's getting warmer day by day.
The arrival of spring.
The cat had moved to another place
Before I knew it.
Although the cat was laying down
On the main road under a car
Every morning around this time last year,
If I remember correctly.
I wonder of the woman in a negligee was
Her owner, as I thought.
Lucky is not here.
Neither is the cat.
I feel lonely this spring.

20 March 1998

窓

小さい窓からは小さい空しか見えない
年々　私の部屋は
だんだん薄暗くなってきている
だんだん小さく　仕舞いに
ポチッとついている
オレンジ色の豆電球は希望かな

部屋の窓も
年々　小さくなっていく
空も　小さくなっていく
向こうの空を飛ぶ鳩の存在も
知らない
流れる雲について
何処から来て　何処へ行くのかさえも
見えない

ただ　分かるのは
風が吹いていることだけ
小さい窓からは小さい空しか見えない

1998.7.25

264

A Window

We can only see a small sky
From a small window.
My room is getting dimmer gradually every year.
Is the orange coloured light bulb which
Became smaller and ended up being a tiny light
My only hope?
The window of my room is growing smaller
Every year.
The sky is also shrinking.
I can't know of the existence of a white dove
That is flying in the other sky.
As for clouds that are floating,
I can't see even where they come from or
Where they are going.
I only know that
The wind is blowing.
We can see only a small sky
From a small window.

25 July 1998

あの人の右手

私の愛するあの人の右手
もし　手に入らないのなら
いっそう　手首から切り取ってしまいましょう

それがどうしても出来ないのなら
せめて　接着剤で
私の左手と
あの人の右手を
ピタリとくっつけてしまいましょう

それすらも出来ないなら
逃げましょう
忘れましょう
泣きましょう

どれも無理な話です

1998.7.25

His Right Hand

The right hand of the person I love.
If I can't have it,
Let's cut it off from the wrist!
If it's really impossible to cut,
Let's stick my left hand to his right hand
Perfectly with glue, at least.
If it's impossible even to glue,
Let's escape!
Let's forget!
Let's cry!
All these things seem to be out of the question.

25 July 1998

光のトンネル

人生は真っ暗なトンネル
先に微かな光が見える
きっと　その光の方向が
進むべき方向で
そこに出口があるのだろう

時には歩いて
時にはスキップ
足元のデコボコさえも見えないが
時折　走ってみたくなる
ザワザワ　人の声を聞きながら
ある時は静かに立ち止まって
風の音を聞いてみる
すると　風は囁く
優しい声で

私は後ろを振り返る
遥か遠く　微かな
消えそうで消えない
白っぽい光が見える

もしかしたら
進むべき方向はこっちなのかも知れない

ううん、
もしかしたら
先に見える光の出口と
この小さな懐かしい光は
つながっているのかも知れない

そうだ
私は戻れるのだ
あの一番幸福だった　あの場所に
ならば　安心して先へ進もうとしよう

　　　　　　　　１９９８.８.２７

A Tunnel of Light

Our life is a dark tunnel.
I can see a faint light ahead.
I am sure that
The direction from which the light is shining is
The direction to which I should go, and
The exit will be there.
I walk sometimes and skip sometimes.
I occasionally want to try running,
Although I can't see the uneven road
Under my feet.
Other times I just stand quietly
Trying to listen to the sound of the wind,
While I hear the sound of people buzzing.
The wind whispers in a gentle voice.
I look back.
I can see the pale light, which seems
So near and yet is so far away.
If I'm not wrong,
The direction to which I must move
May be this way.

No, perhaps the exit the light shows
And this small familiar light
May connect to each other.
Yes, I can return.
I can return to the happiest place
Where I once was.
Then I will go forward without fear.

27 August 1998

目薬

青い炎がチラチラと
黄色い光がユラユラと
桃色の液体は　あと僅か
あと一回分
チラチラ　ユラユラ見えるのは
私の目が頑張っているからなんだ

1998.10.7

Eye Drops

A blue blaze is shimmering.
A yellow light is swaying.
There is a little more of the pink liquid.
One more portion.
I can see chira chira, yura yura
Because my eyes are doing their best.

7 October 1998

太陽と地球説

あの人は太陽
私は地球

偉大なる太陽の引力に引っ張られて
私は太陽の周りを　クルクル回る
太陽に近づこうとすると
熱い　汗をかく
火傷をするので近づけない

太陽の周りを　クルクル回っていることが
辛いと感じても
逃げ出すことは出来ない

6分の1の引力の月は
突然　私の前に現れて
私の周りを　いそいそ回って
飛んでいく
別の月も突然現れて
いそいそ回って
また　飛んでいく

もっと大きな月が現れて
太陽の前に立ちはだかってくれたら
私は太陽の引力から
逃げることが出来るのに

これも宇宙の法則
自然の摂理
あぁ　太陽は偉大だ

　　　　　　1998.10.8

A Doctrine about the Sun and the Earth

That person is the Sun.
I am the Earth.
I orbit around the Sun: kuru kuru.
I move thus by the gravitational power of
The great Sun.
If I am about to come too close to the Sun,
I feel hot and sweat.
I must not come too close to the Sun
Because I would be scalded.
I can't escape from this situation
Even though I feel it to be very hard
For me to orbit around the Sun: kuru kuru.
The Moon, with one sixth of the gravity of the Earth
Suddenly appeared in front of me and
Swiftly flew around me and then flew away.
Another moon suddenly appeared
And also flew around me hurriedly.
I believe that I can escape

From the gravitational pull of the Sun
If a larger moon appears and
Stands in front of the Sun.
This is the law of the Universe.
This is Mother Nature.
Oh, the Sun is great.

8 October 1998

太陽と地球の位置関係

太陽と地球の位置関係は
精神世界
物理的に接近しても
汗はかくけど
火傷はしない
火傷をするのは
精神世界において
近づき過ぎた時

太陽が近づけば
地球は一歩下がり
地球が二歩近づけば
太陽は三歩下がる

これ　宇宙の法則
自然の摂理
精神世界
太陽と地球は
距離を保たねばならない
運命ともいうのだろうか

１９９８.１０.８

278

The Position between the Sun and the Earth

The position between the Sun and the Earth
Is inner space.
Even if they approach each other physically,
They are not burned and just sweat.
They are burned when they are close to one another mentally.
If the Sun comes close,
The Earth moves away one step.
If the Earth takes two steps closer,
The Sun backs away three steps.
This is a rule of the Universe.
This is Mother Nature.
This is inner space.
The Sun and the Earth must keep their distance.
Should I say that this is their fate?

8 October 1998

桃色の湯たんぽ

小さく硬くなったお前の体を
じっと見つめながら
おはよう
おやすみ
行ってきます
ただいま
繰り返す

あの時　桃色の湯たんぽの上に
お前をちょこんと乗せておけば
お前は死ぬことはなかった
後悔は憂鬱を引き起こす
あの時に戻れたらと願う
お風呂に入った後のお前の体は
柔らかく　とても綺麗で
少し笑っているようだった

おはよう
おやすみ
行ってきます
ただいま

繰り返される挨拶は
後悔の表れ
お前に謝りたい気持ち

１９９８．１２．２４

A Pink Hot-water Bottle

"Ohayou,
Oyasumi,
Ittekimasu,
Tadaima"
I repeat, gazing at your small hard body.
You would not have died
If I had let you lay on the pink hot-water bottle.
Regret causes depression.
I wish I could go back to the time when...
Your body was soft and clean and
You smiled a little
After you had taken a bath
"Ohayou,
Oyasumi,
Ittekimasu,
Tadaima"

Those greetings, which I repeat, are my regret.
They are my feelings of wanting to apologize to you.

24 December 1998

セブンアップ

缶の中に　Ｌｕｃｋｙちゃんがいる
多分　もうすぐ一年になるから
私に会いに来てくれたのだろう
キュッキュッと鳴く声は
とても懐かしい

透明な炭酸水は　生命の水
生まれては消えて
Ｌｕｃｋｙちゃんも
生まれては消えて
死んでしまった

Ｌｕｃｋｙちゃんはプチッと生まれ
パチンッと消えた

缶の中にｌｕｃｋｙちゃんがいる
沢山いる

１９９９．２．１９

Seven-up

Lucky-chan is inside a tin can.
Maybe he came to visit me
Because one year will soon have passed.
His voice: kyu kyu, is very familiar to me.
Transparent soda water is the water for life.
They were born and then disappeared.
Lucky-chan was also born and then died.
Lucky-chan was born: puchi, and then
Disappeared: pachin.
There are a lot of Lucky-chans
Inside the tin can.

19 February 1999

もぐらの私

二月末
もぐらは地下のねぐらに閉じこもる
ジメジメした中で考える
将来のこと
お金のこと
家族のこと

Luckyのこと
好きな人のこと・・・

三月一日
母は何でもお見通し
雨の中　一番小さなもぐらが迷子になり
ねぐらに帰って来ない夢を見た
と連絡あり

三月二日　午前6時
久しぶりに地上に出てみれば
空は朝だった
これは春の仕業だ
いつの間に春が来たんだろうと思いながら
ねぐらへ戻る
春の日差しは眩しいものだ

1999.3.2

286

I AM A MOLE

(The end of February)

A mole shut herself into her lair in the basement.
She was thinking about her future and her money.
Her family, Lucky, her lover...
Inside the damp lair.

(The first of March).
Her Mother could see through everything.
She told her daughter that she had dreamt
About the smallest mole, who had lost her way
And hasn't come home.

(The second of March, 6:00 AM).
It was a morning sky
When the mole came out of the ground,
After a while.
This was the work of spring.
She returned to her lair, wondering, when spring came.
The spring sunshine will be sparkling.

2 March 1999

桜の言うこと

桜新町の桜はユッサユサ
ユッサユサ　ユッサユサと
揺れながら
重い頭を垂らして
通りの人並みを眺めている

この時代の人間は
何故　あぁも　くたびれているのだろう
どうして　こんなに
しかめっ面をしているのだろうか

桜の木達は
隣同士で話している
そして

人間達よ
空を眺めよ　透明な風の音を聞き
本当に美しく大切なものを悟れよ

と語り掛ける
しかし　人間は気付かない
夢中でセカセカと歩いているのだ

1999.4.17

MESSAGES FROM CHERRY BLOSSOMS

Cherry Blossoms trees in Sakurashin-machi are
Weeping with their heavy heads and
Viewing people on the street,
Swaying: yussa yusa, yussa yusa, yussa yusa.
Why do the people of this age look so tired like that?
Why do so many people frown with faces like this?
Cherry Blossom trees are talking next to each other.
And they try to speak to us.
Dear people,
Look at the sky!
Listen to the sound of the lucid wind
And sense what really beautiful and important beings they are!
However, people don't notice these things.
They are too busy walking hurriedly without looking up.

17 April 1999

桜の木の下で

桜は花を咲かせ
散ってしまっても
また見事な姿を見せるでしょう

季節は廻り
寒い冬の後に
暖かな春の訪れがやってくるでしょう

真っ暗な夜があっても
日はまた昇り
朝が来る

でも　あの人はいない
全ては同じ繰り返し
でも　あの人はいない
あの人はいってしまった

同じ繰り返しの中で
一生は儚く
だから　尊いものであると
感じざるを得ません

一生懸命　生きて
全てのものに優しさと
いたわりの気持ちを持つことを
気付かせてくれるもの
それが生命の終わりである

　　　　　１９９９.５.１４

Under Cherry Blossoms

Cherry Blossom trees will show us
Their wonderful figures again
Even though their petals drop after blooming.
The arrival of warm spring comes
After freezing winter
Because each of the seasons return.
The Sun rises again and the dawn comes
No matter how dark is the night we endure.
Yet, a certain person is not here.
All things are repeated but that person is not here.
The person has passed away.
I can't help but feel that
Our lifetime, in the same pattern of repetition is
Fragile, therefore, it is precious.

It's a thing that enables us to recognize
That we should live doing our utmost and
Show kindness and consideration for all.
It is the end of our life.

14 May 1999

日曜日　午前5時

みんなはもう夏休みになったのかな
梅雨はもう明けたのかな
大きい雲は　何処　行くのかな
私は月曜日から
また　しゃんと生きられるのかな

1999.7.18

Sunday, Five PM

I wonder if they have already been on
Their summer holiday.
I wonder if the rainy season has already ended.
I wonder where the big cloud will go.
I wonder if I can live, as I'm my own man
Again from Monday.

18 July 1999

カニの気持ち　－６月のパーティーにて－

カニＡ「お願いだ！私を家に帰しておくれ・・・
　　　　ブクブクブク・・・」
カニＢ「私には妻も子供もいるのだ！死ぬわけに
　　　　はいかぬのだ・・・ブクブクブク・・・」
カニＣ「お願いだ！逃がしてくれ・・・ブクブク
　　　　ブク・・・」

（台所にて）
カニＡ「あぁ、あの広い海に帰りたいなぁ〜。
　　　　シュー（油の中に入っていく）」
カニＢ「今度生まれ変われるとしたら、それでも、
　　　　私はまたカニがいいなぁ〜。シュー
　　　　（油の中に入っていく）」
カニＣ「私も人間なんかには絶対生まれないぞ！
　　　　シュー（油の中に入っていく）」

（テーブルの上にて）
隣のエビフライ「君たちは、まだいいよ。私は
　　　　　　　　ここに来る前から、頭や手足を
　　　　　　　　もぎ取られていたので、初めか
　　　　　　　　らエビフライとしてしか見ても
　　　　　　　　らえなかった。」

カニＡ・Ｂ・Ｃ「うん、うん。」
隣のエビフライ「私の海老としての尊厳や命の
　　　　　　　尊さなんて、ましてや哀れみ
　　　　　　　なんて私には全く無縁のもの
　　　　　　　だった。それを考えたら、君た
　　　　　　　ちなんてまだ幸せだっただろ？」
カニＡ・Ｂ・Ｃ「本当にそうだ。エビさんが
　　　　　　　可哀想だ。では、私達も潔く
　　　　　　　黙って食べられるとしよう。」
一同「この世の中は全く理不尽なものだ！！」
　　　　　　　　　　１９９９．７．１８

THE CRABS' FEELINGS
(AT A PARTY IN JUNE)

Crab A: "Please let me go home...*buku, buku,buku*..."

Crab B: " I have a wife and children.

   I must not die here... *buku, buku, buku*..."

Crab C: "Please let us go... *buku, buku, buku*..."

(In a kitchen)

Crab A: "Oh, I want to return to the huge sea..."

   Shuu (the sound of him being put into boiling oil).

Crab B: "I wish that I will be born as a crab again.

   If I could be reborn next..."

   Shuu (the sound of him being put into boiling oil).

Crab C: "I wouldn't like to be born as a human!"

   Shuu (the sound of him being put into boiling oil).

(On a table)

Neighboring deep-fried prawn:

"You were luckier than me.

I have been recognized as an only deep-fried prawn from the beginning because my head and hands had already been mutilated before I came here."

Crabs A, B, and C: "Yes, yes."

Neighboring deep-fried prawn:

"I was completely devoid of dignity as a prawn. I was given no respect, much less sympathy. If you compare you and me, you will say that you were still luckier, won't you?"

Crabs A, B, and C: "Yes, you are right! Poor prawn... Okay then, let's be eaten with moaning, gracefully!"

All: "This world is totally absurd!!"

18 July 1999

夕立

ビリビリと空の彼方に
金色のひびが入り
しばらく経って
ドドド・・・と鈍い音がする

空気が重くなり
心臓がドキドキし
どっと汗が出る

いつの間にか
黒い巨大なモンスターは
空一帯を覆い
私達を苦しめる

鳥達は家路を急ぎ
不安な心を隠せない

毎度やって来る
こんな夏の風物詩だけれど
懐かしい香りがするのは
何故だろう

1999.7.21

300

LATE AFTERNOON SHOWER

A golden crack appears: *biri biri*
In the far-beyond-sky and
It sounds: do, do, do...deadly after a while.
The air becomes heavier.
My heart beats: *doki doki* and
The sweat pours off my body.
The black vast monster covers
The whole sky before we know it and
Torments us.
Birds hurry home and
They can't hide their uneasy feelings.
I am wondering why it smells familiar.
Although it is a kind of summer
Scene, which comes over every year.

21 July 1999

夏のスクーリング

揺らめくアスファルト
木々の隙間から降り注ぐフラッシュ
緑の風が動き
簡素な教室にいる私
全ては一瞬の光景なのだ

世界の空から眺めたら
私はただのちっぽけな存在
宇宙から見たら
いないも同然だ

長い時間の中で
私の人生は点のようなもの
大変辛い苦しみも
ただの一瞬の出来事なのだ
辛くて泣いても
不安で怯えても
気が付けば
もう戻れない一瞬なのだ

思い出となったものを
振り返れば
既に懐かしく
失った時と考えれば
あんなに嫌がった時でさえも
もう一度戻りたくなる

壊れやすいガラス細工のような人生
私は時間のエスカレーターに乗り
幾度となく振り返るのだ

1999.7.30

Summer Schooling

It is a wavering asphalt road.
It is a flashlight, which pours light between trees.
The flow of a green wind.
It is me who is in a plain classroom.
Everything is a scene for a split second.
If you look at me from the sky all over the world,
I am just a tiny being.
If you look at me from the Universe,
I am almost the same as nothing.
My lifetime looks like a dot in a long time line.
Even very heavy agony is a mere momentary event.
Even though I cry from the pain and worry with fears,
It becomes a moment to which I cannot go back
When I noticed.
If I look back at the things which
Became my memory,
They are good old already.

If I think of it as the time that I lost,
I will be eager to return once more
In spite of the time when I was so reluctant.
It is my life, like a fragile work of glass.
I often look back on the time escalator.

30 July 1999

ある日　電気を直して思ったこと

ある日　電気を直して思ったこと
虫の死骸がいっぱいあって

ギャーッてなって

ほこりまみれになって

汗まみれになって
手が真っ黒になって

こんなこと
他の大人がやってくれればいいのにって
ちょっと思って

それでも
再び明かりが点いた時は
嬉しくて

エヘンッとなって

生きるって大変なんだなぁー

1999.9.1

306

My Thoughts after I fixed a Light on the day

There is a thing that I thought
When I fixed the light on the day.
There were a lot of insect carcasses, and
I was frightened by them.
I was covered with dust and sweat,
My hands were very dirty,
I wished a little that other adults could help
Me with tasks such as these;
Yet, I was very happy and proud of myself
When the light was on again.
It's really tough to stay alive.

1 September 1999

地下鉄のホーム

都会の中の静けさは
怖い位の貴重な空間

初めて未開の地に
足を踏み入れるように
恐る恐る歩く足音だけが
鳴り響く

地下鉄のホームの5秒間
ちょっとした
安堵感があった

1999.10.23

A Platform on the Subway

Silence in a city is
Such a precious thing that I'm afraid.
Only the sound of my own footfall as I timidly walk
As if I stepped into unexplored territory
For the first time, echoes.
Five seconds on a subway platform.
There was little relief.

23 October 1999

白い月

秋
白い月を見つけたら
雲も同じ色だった
　（あぁ　綺麗だなー）
顔を上向きにして眺めたら
清々しかった
　（あぁ　気持ちいいなー）
横道に入ってから　また眺めたら
背筋がスゥーとして
また気持ちよかった
　（この秋に何処か行きたいなー）
白い月を見て
私の目や身体は喜んでいるようだ
　（のんびり連れて行ってあげたいなー）

　　　　　　　　　　１９９９.１１.１

A WHITE MOON

Autumn.
When I found a white moon,
I found clouds of the same colour.
"Oh, it's beautiful!"
When I viewed them closer,
I felt refreshed.
"Oh, I feel so good!"
When I turned into a path and looked up again,
I felt so nice again
Because I stretched my back.
"I would like to go somewhere this autumn."
My eyes and body seemed happy
Thanks to the white moon.
"I want to take myself off to relax somewhere."

1 November 1999

０．０５mmのプランクトン

暗黒な夜の海に光るプランクトン
０．０５mmの生命
小さな小さな輝き
過酷でもあり優しくもある
この世界の中で
精一杯生きる単細胞
まことに小さく光るプランクトン

それは　私
それは静かな生命の存在

　　　　　　　　　２０００.3.12

0.05 MM PLANKTON

Shining plankton in the dark night sea.
0.05 mm life.
It is a tiny sparkle that could be both
Severe and gentle.
It is a single-celled organism that has a hard life
In this world.
Very small shining plankton.
It's me.
It is the existence of silent life.

12 March 2000

臆病な赤ちゃん

臆病な赤ちゃんは
朝　目が覚めても
瞼を開くことが出来ません

ずっとずっと
夢を見続けていたいのです

この世界の光が差し込むと
またこの世界で生き
また毎日の生活を
繰り返さなければならないのです

臆病な赤ちゃんは
何か不安を感じて
目を閉じたまま
外の様子を伺います

そして　無意味な一日の始まり
朝を迎えるのです

2000.7.24

314

A Timid Baby

In the morning
A timid baby can't open her eyes
Even though she has woken up.
She prefers to continue dreaming forever.
She has to live in this world again and
Repeat her daily life again
When the world's light floods her eyes.
The timid baby observes the outside world
Without opening her eyes
Because she feels anxiety.
And the day begins meaninglessly.
Thus she receives the morning.

24 July 2000

あの夏へ帰ろう

あの夏へ帰ろう
まだ何も考えず
まだ何の不安や責任もなかった
あの夏へ帰ろう

夏の暑い日
私は自分の人生を歩き出した
それは今ここへ来る為の
入り口だった
何も考えず　扉を叩いた
何も知らず　扉を開いた

もう長く歩き過ぎて
入り口は見えなくなってしまった
もう帰れない

帰れないと分かりつつ
また思ってしまう
あの夏へ帰ろう

2000.8.3

LET'S RETURN TO THAT SUMMER

Let's return to that summer!
Let's go back to that summer
When I hadn't thought anything yet or
I hadn't any anxiety or responsibilities
At all…yet!
On that hot summer day
I started waking on my own.
It was the entrance for me to come here now.
I knocked at the door without thinking.
I opened the door with my innocence.
I can no longer see the entrance
Because I walked away so long ago.
I can't return there anymore.
I know that I can't return
But I wish again that I could.
Let's return to that summer.

3 August 2000

ハエよ

苦しいか　苦しいか
お前は何の為に生まれて来たんだい
一体　何処から入って来たのかい

お前の霧の中の
苦しそうな叫び声を聞くと
お前にも 尊い生命があることに気付かされ
また　その声を最後まで仕留めなければならんと
複雑な緊張が汗を呼ぶ

戦争
そう　戦争
これは小さなジャングルで起こった
小さな戦争なのだ

　　　　　　　　2000.9.2

A Fly

Are you choking? Are you choking?
Why were you born?
Where on earth did you enter from?
When I heard you cry with pain in the spray,
I realized that you also had your precious life.
Also, complex tension caused me to sweat
Because I had to nail you until the last voice.
A war.
Yes, a war.
This is a small war that took place
In a small jungle.

2 September 2000

洋菓子とゴキブリ

甘い洋菓子の欠片を
こぼしながら食べる人間
トボトボと
近付いて来るミクロなゴキブリ
そう　それはまるで
オアシスを探し求めて歩く
異邦人

この欠片をあげてもいいけど
君はもうすぐいなくなる
私の手によって
君は殺されるのだから
あげることは出来ないよ

もう食欲がなくなってきた
早く何処か行ってくれ

２０００.１０.６

A Cake and a Cockroach

A human eating a sweet cake,
Dropping pieces of it.
A micro-sized cockroach that plods on
To be close to the crumbs.
Yes, it looks like a foreigner who
Walks around, looking for an oasis.
Though I can give you this piece of cake,
You will disappear soon.
I can't give it to you
Because you will be killed by these hands of mine.
I have lost my appetite.
Please go away at once.

6 October 2000

我が道を行こう

出来ることは一生懸命努力しよう
気が付いたことはやろう
人を妬むのはやめよう
羨むこともやめよう
イライラもやめよう
でも　好きなようにやろう
楽しくいこう

私達はこの雨や太陽
空や雲や　虹や風
地球という生命体の中で
生きている

この大自然と調和しながら
我が道を行こう

２０００.１１.１１

I'll Go My Own Way

Let's make an effort, as much as possible!
Let's do it when we recognize what we should do.
Let's stop envying others.
Let's stop being jealous as well!
Let's stop being irritated!
However, let's also do what we really want to do!
I will enjoy my life!
We live in the rain and the sunshine,
The sky, the clouds, the rainbows, and the wind,
Including an animated body whose
Name is the Earth.
Let's do it our way,
Harmonizing with glorious Nature.

11 November 2000

大きな虹を思い出せ

ちっちゃいことを気にするな

つまらないことでイライラするな

雨が降ったら　止むのを待つしかない

嵐が来たら　濡れるしかない

病気になったら　治るのを待つしかない

天気が良かったら　神の思し召しと思うだけ

この世の中　自分の力では

どうしようも出来ないことが沢山ある

細かいことを気にするな

イライラした時は

あの雨の日を思い出せ

あの大きな虹を思い出せ

後は　なるようになる

きっと　何とかなるのだから

2000.11.11

324

Remember the Big Rainbow

Don't be bothered by tiny things.
Don't be irritated by trifling matters.
We only have to wait until it stops
If it's raining.
There is no other choice but to be wet
If a storm comes.
All we can do is to wait and recover
If we become sick.
If the weather is good
We should just accept that it is the will of Heaven.
There are a lot of things that we can't control in this world.
Don't trouble yourself about unimportant matters.
When you are annoyed
Remember the rainy day.
Remember the big rainbow.
Things will be as they should be afterwards.
I'm sure that they will be as they should be.

11 November 2000

夢から覚めた時のように

夢から覚めた時のように
全ては一瞬のうちに消えてしまう

昨日までの生活
楽しい笑い声
苦々しく思ったこと
パンの焼ける匂い
あの道　あの低い空

全てはブラックホールに吸い込まれて
何事もなかったかのように
再び始まる
そう　夢から覚めた時のように
２ヵ月もの間　私は眠り続け
今　目覚めたかのように

２０００.１２.９

It Seems Like When I Awake from a Dream

Everything disappears in a moment,
As if I just awoke from a dream.
Life until yesterday,
Happy laughter.
Things that disgusted me.
The smell of toast.
That street, the low sky of England.
All is swallowed up in the black hole and
My daily life restarts
As if nothing happened.
It seems as if I awoke from a dream.
It seems like I woke up now
After I had slept
For two months.

9 December 2000

<ruby>豆電球<rt>まめでんきゅう</rt></ruby>

オレンジ<ruby>色<rt>いろ</rt></ruby>の
<ruby>古<rt>ふる</rt></ruby>く<ruby>懐<rt>なつ</rt></ru9かしい
<ruby>惨<rt>みじ</rt></ruby>めな
でも　<ruby>温<rt>あたた</rt></ruby>かい
<ruby>幸<rt>しあわ</rt></ruby>せな
<ruby>静<rt>しず</rt></ruby>かな<ruby>夜<rt>よる</rt></ruby>の<ruby>光<rt>ひかり</rt></ruby>

<ruby>私<rt>わたし</rt></ruby>はどうなってしまうのだろう
お<ruby>父<rt>とう</rt></ruby>さん　お<ruby>母<rt>かあ</rt></ruby>さん
<ruby>私<rt>わたし</rt></ruby>はどうなってしまうのでしょうね

２００１．１．２９

A MINIATURE BULB

It is orange colored,
Old, familiar,
Miserable,
But it is a warm and happy
Light from a silent night.
What's going on with me?
Father, Mother,
What will happen to me?

29 January 2001

バスの中で

え？え？
お金より大切なもの
勉強より大事なこと
自分のことより大切にすべきもの
何か分かりかけてきたような
何か掴みかけてきたような

あっ　あ、
だから　眠れなかったんだ
だから　私に行かせたんだ
私にそれを悟らせようとしたのかな

イライラが消えてきた

バスの一番前の椅子に座る代わりに
ご褒美として
帰りに二子玉のたこ焼きを買って帰ろう
　　　　　　　　　　　2001.2.9

IN A BUS

What? What?
Is it more valuable than money?
Is it more important than studying?
Is it what I should take care of more than myself?
I feel that I am on my way to understanding something.
I feel that I nearly get it.
Oh, yes!
That's why I had to go.
I wonder if God tried to make me realize that.
My impatience is fading away.
I'll buy Tako-yaki in Nikotama for my reward
On my way home
Instead of sitting on the first front seat of a bus.

9 February 2001

桜と刀

月 風 花びら

酒 刀 侍

龍馬もこの道を歩いたのかな

あまりに綺麗だから

今日だけは争いをやめて

一緒に飲もうよ

あの先の屋台で

2001.4.30

Cherry Blossoms and a Sword

The moon, wind, petals.
Sake, sword, samurai,
I wonder if Ryouma also walked upon this street.
Let's stop the battles and have a drink together,
Just today,
Because tonight is so beautiful!
At the booth ahead of us.

30 April 2001

小さな窓の外

窓の外から
小さな鳥が私に話し掛ける

お元気ですか？
調子はどうですか？

空気の入れ替えは
心の入れ替え
新鮮な風が
私の心の中に入ってくる
天気が良いし
今日は何をしようかな

2001.5.15

334

Outside a Small Window

A little bird talks to me
From outside a window.
"How are you?
How are things?"
To change the air is to snap out of it.
Fresh wind comes into my heart.
It's a lovely day today.
So, what shall I do today?

15 May 2001

涙の理由

私が求めているものは何？

地位　名誉　お金

若さ　美しさ　健康

家族　友達　恋人

生き甲斐　キャリア

美味しい食べ物・・・

幸せってどうしたら感じるの？

何か満たされない心はどうしてなの？

気が付けば、私は＊＊＊＊になっていた

（＊＊＊＊の中に好きな言葉を入れよ）

２００１．４．３０

336

THE REASON FOR THE TEARS

What am I looking for?
Position, honour, money,
Youth, beauty, health,
Family, friends, a boyfriend.
Salt of my life, a career,
Home, delicious food...
What should I do to feel happy?
Why can't I feel satisfaction?
When I realized
I had already become...
(Complete the last sentence with your own word).

30 April 2001

海の底の箱

人の心は小さな箱のようなもの
誰も覗くことは出来ない
時折　光が差し込まない
深くて暗い海底へ沈んで行く

静かな静かな海の底
誰にもその扉を開けることは出来ない
自然にプカプカ浮き上がり
太陽の下で扉が開く時
また　いつもの笑顔が見られることだろう

2001.9.8

338

A Box on the Seabed

Our hearts are like a small box.
Nobody can look inside.
At times the box is sinking to
The bottom of a deep dark sea that
The sunlight doesn't reach.
Silent silent seabed.
Nobody can open the door of the box.
We can see an ordinary smile again
When it comes to the surface
Naturally: puka puka,
And the door opens under the sun.

8 September2001

もし　死にたいなと思ったら

死んでしまいたい
そう思ってみても　もう一人の私が言う
そんなことで死んじゃだめだ！
そんなちっぽけなことで死んでしまったら
可哀想だ！

長い時間の中で
たったちょっとの今だけなのに
今　あなたがひっそりと死んでしまったなら
誰もあなたが死んだことに気付かない
あなたという人間は　今も昔も
この世の中で　たった一人だというのに
そのたった一人の尊いあなたが死んでしまっても
誰も気付かない
長い歴史の中で
あなたという尊い人間が生きたことは
ほとんどの人は知らない
知らないままで　あなたは死んでゆく

あなたが生きていることを
もっと教えてあげよう
あなたが自然に死んでゆく時
あなたの為に本当に泣いてくれる人が
もっと　いる

探<ruby>探<rt>さが</rt></ruby>しに行<ruby>行<rt>い</rt></ruby>こう
それからでも遅<ruby>遅<rt>おそ</rt></ruby>くない
いつか　最後<ruby>最後<rt>さいご</rt></ruby>は誰<ruby>誰<rt>だれ</rt></ruby>にでもやって来<ruby>来<rt>く</rt></ruby>るのだから

　　　　　　　　　２００１．９．１７

If You Think that You Want to Die

"I want to die."
Even though I am thinking this thought, another part of me says:
"No, you should not die because of such a thing!
It would be a pity for you
If you died for such a tiny reason!"
The present is just a mere moment
In a long expanse of time.
If you died quietly now,
Nobody would notice your death.
Even though you are the only one in this world
Now at this moment,
Even if you, who are precious and unique, were to die,
Nobody would notice it.
Most people don't know that
You, who are such a precious person, have lived
For a long time in human history.
You are going to die before they know you.
Let's tell them more about your existence.
When you pass away naturally
Then there will be more people who will cry
From the bottom of their hearts for you.

Let's go to look for those people!
It won't be too late then
Because the end will visit everyone, without fail.

17 September 2001

心の色

空を見上げてごらん
空は何色？
雲は流れてる？
風は何か囁いてる？

もし　空がどんよりと
グレーの雲に覆われていたら
あなたの心はセピア色

心がセピア色になった時
色を付けてあげるよ
どこからか　声が聞こえる

花は何色？
甘い香りはする？
赤　白　黄　桃　橙　紫・・・
沢山の花が咲き乱れてる？
虹は何色？
求めて止まない幸せの色
あなたの心は　今　何色？

2002.3.28

344

The Colour of a Heart

Look up at the sky.
What colour is the sky?
Are there clouds floating in the sky?
Is the wind whispering?
If the sky is covered by dull gray clouds,
Your heart will be sepia coloured.
"When you have a sepia heart,
I will make the colour for you."
I hear the voice from somewhere.
What colour are the flowers?
Do they smell sweet?
Red, white, yellow, pink, orange, purple...
Do many flowers bloom?
What colours does a rainbow show?
Colours of happiness, which we can't but ask for.
What colour is your heart now?

28 March 2002

桜の傘

雨　しとしと
雨　しとしと
セットした髪が乱れます

ちょいと
この傘にお入りなさいな
こちらの傘にも
こっちにも・・・

どうもありがとう
お陰で濡れずに済みました

優しい桜新町の桜の木
誰も持っていない
大きなピンクの傘でした

２００２.４.１１

CHERRY BLOSSOM UMBRELLA

Rain: *shito, shito.*
Rain: *shito, shito.*
My hair was just done, and now it's getting tousled and wet.
"Excuse me,
Why don't you come under this umbrella?"
"Come under this umbrella as well."
"This one too."
Thank you very much.
I didn't get wet, thanks to you.
Gentle cherry blossom trees in Sakaurashimmachi.
They were big pink umbrellas such as no one else has.

11 April 2002

京都の眠れない夜

一生懸命　生きよう

遊ぶ時は遊んで
休む時は休んで
学ぶ時は学んで
動く時は動いて
力の限り　頑張ろう

楽しい時は楽しく
楽しくない時も楽しく

一生懸命　生きよう

2002.4.14

348

A Sleepless Night in Kyoto

I want to live, doing my best.
I'll enjoy it when I am having fun.
I'll relax when I'm taking a rest.
I'll study hard when I am learning.
I'll work hard when I work.
Let's make an effort, as much as possible.
Be happy when it is a happy time.
Also, be happy when it is a time of unhappiness.
I want to live, doing my utmost.

14 April 2002

桜咲くとき、星が輝くとき

桜　咲く
来年も咲く
でも　人の命は永遠ではない

星　輝く
何億光年　輝く
でも　人の命は儚い

風は歌い
雲は流れる
人の命は何処へ行く

あなたはどう感じますか
あなたはどう生きますか

形ある物はいつかは壊れ
命ある者はいつかは亡くなる
それが世の中の無常

あなたはどう感じますか
あなたはどう生きますか

２００２.６.１

350

WHEN CHERRY BLSOM TREES BLOOM
WHEN STARS TWINKLE

Cherry blossom trees bloom.
They will bloom next year as well.
However, our lives are not so eternal.
Stars twinkle.
They will twinkle for many millions of years.
However, our lives are fragile.
The wind sings and the clouds float.
Where will our lives go to?
How do you feel?
How do you live?
Things will lose their form someday.
That which is animate, which has life, will pass away someday.
Everything is mutable in this world.
How do you feel?
How do you live?

1 June 2002

絶対、健康になるからね

絶対　健康になるからね
そう言って
彼女は南の島へ旅立って行った

見知らぬ所へ行く
期待と不安
まだ何1つとして
実を結んでいない彼女の
ささやかな願い
明るく笑った最後の言葉

今　彼女はどうしているだろう
あれから　どうなったのだろう
南の風に聞いてみようか
今　彼女は幸せかな

２００２.7.14

I Promise to be Healthy, Without Fail

I will promise to be healthy, without fail.
She started for a south island
After she had said this.
Expectation and fear, going to an unfamiliar place.
Her small wish, which has borne no fruit yet.
It was the last word she spoke with her bright smile.
I'm wondering how she is doing now
And what happened to her afterwards.
Shall I ask the south wind about her?
Is she happy now?

14 July 2002

茶ナマコの気持ち

ちょっと　折角　くつろいでるんやから
邪魔せんといてや！
ブバーッ
邪魔する奴はこれでもくらえ！！
ネバネバ攻撃や

わしら　動かへんし
大人しいと思ったら
大間違いやで！
馬鹿にすんのも　ええ加減にしとき！

カニちゃんだって
砂の中でブクブク言いながら
早く行け！と思っとるし
綺麗なブルーの子供魚だって
あんたらをからかってるだけやで

とにかく　邪魔せんといて！
頼みますわ　ほんまに

２００２.７.１４

A Brown Sea Cucumber's Feelings

Excuse me,
Please don't disturb me because
I am relaxed, as I expected to be!
Bubaaaa!
Take this, distraction!
Neba neba attack!
You may think that we are passive
Because you can't see us move,
But you are making a big mistake!
Give me a break and stop making fun of us!
Crabs are also thinking, "Get away!"
Making bubbles, buku buku in the sand
And beautiful blue fish children are
Just teasing you as well.
Anyway, don't disturb us, please!
Seriously!!

14 July 2002

苦しいこと　楽しいこと

楽しいことは楽しいことではなく
苦しいことは苦しいことではない
なぜなら
楽しいことは一瞬であり
苦しいこともまた一瞬だからである
別れを告げる時
それは真の楽しいこととなり
それは真の苦しいこととなるのだろう

　　　　　　　　　　　　２００２.８.２７

AGONY AND PLEASURE

Pleasure is not pleasure and
Agony is not agony.
That's because pleasure lasts for a split second
And agony also lasts for a split second.
When you say good-bye
It will be a real pleasure and
It will be a real agony.

27 August 2002

秋の夕暮れ

白い半月の空を飛ぶよ
この帽子
その帽子
あの帽子
トンボは止まって伝えてくれる

秋が来たよ
鈴虫が鳴くよ
ススキが揺れるよ
空が高いよ

向こうの田んぼを見てごらん
夕日が照らして綺麗だね
秋の夕暮れは淋しいから
もう帰ろう
風に吹かれて
もう帰ろうよ

2002.10.13

Autumn Twilight

They fly in the sky of a white half-moon.
This cap,
That cap,
The cap over there.
Dragonflies tell us, landing on our heads:
"Autumn came."
"Bell-ringing crickets will sing."
"Japanese pampas grass will wave."
"The sky is high."
Look at the rice paddies over there.
They are so beautiful
Because the twilight sun lightens them.
Let's go home,
As the autumn dusk makes us feel lonely.
Let's go back home,
Blown by the wind.

13 October 2002

駅員さんの長い一日

駅員さん、駅員さん
今日は一年に一度の大忙しの日
ホームのオレンジ色の電灯が
バツの悪そうな顔を照らし出す

"電車が参りました。一両です。"
"えっ、一両！？"

大勢のお客さんの様々な声
駅員さんは群集に背を向けて
落ちていく夕日を眺めた

今日も日が暮れる

2002.10.13

360

A Station Master's Long Day

A station master, a station master,
Today is the busiest day of the year.
The orange light on a platform illuminated his awkward face.
"The next train came,
Consisting of a single carriage."
"What? Only one carriage...!?"
Various voices from many passengers.
The station master showed his back to the crowd and
Viewed the setting sun.
Today was also drawing to an end.

13 October 2002

菊ケ浜

松陰先生が砂浜を歩いていると
空から大きな龍が言いました

この海のように
青くて広い世界が
早く始まるとええのう

そうじゃのう　塾の者がやってくれるじゃろ

そう言って　松陰先生は
眩しく光る海を見つめました
そして　指月山の方へ向かいました

大きい龍も　また
ワハハと大きい声で笑いながら
指月山の上を飛んで行きました

2002.12.22

KIKUGAHAMA

When Master Shouin was walking on the beach,
A big dragon said from the sky:
"It would be very nice
If the blue and broad world, like this sea, started soon."
"Yes, it would be. My pupils will make it."
Master Shouin gazed at the sea,
Which was shining brilliantly after he made that statement.
And he headed to Mount Shizuki.
The big dragon also flew above Mount Shizuki,
Laughing in a loud voice: "Wa ha ha!"

22 December 2002

下関の鯨

私は下関の鯨
今は丘の上にいるが
昔はよく関門海峡を
行ったり来たりしたもんじゃ

私が泳ぐと
外国の大きな船でさえも
嵐のように揺られ
のんびり浮かんではいられなかった
慌てふためく様を見るのは
とても楽しいものじゃった

今は　毎日　落ちる夕日を丘から眺め
灯るポチポチとした
街の明かりを見ながら
日本も平和になったものだ
と、思うばかりじゃ

2002.12.22

A Whale in Shimonoseki

I am a whale in Shimonoseki.
Though I am on a hill now,
I often used to swim around the Kanmon Strait.
When I swam
Even foreign ships were rocked,
As if a storm had come,
And they could not float leisurely.
I would really enjoy watching those who were very upset.
Now I view the setting sun everyday.
I am just thinking that Japan became peaceful,
Looking at the lights,
Which are like speckles in the town.

22 December 2002

東京の夜

高いビル
賑やかな灯り
沢山の人々

でも　私は一握りの人しか
知らない
また　その人達も
私を知らない

東京の夜
淋しい秋の夜
流れる光を見ながら
私は独りぼっちなんだなぁと思う

2002.12.22

Tokyo Night

Skyscrapers.
Lively illumination.
Many people.
However, I know only a few of them.
And the others also don't know me.
Tokyo night.
Lonely autumn night.
I feel that I am alone,
Looking at the passing illumination.

22 December 2002

あんなに近くにいたのに

あんなに近くにいたのに
手を伸ばせば触れることが出来るその距離は
途中から異空間だったのかもしれない
毎日　見たいと望む夢が
目の前に映し出されただけ

確かに　笑って、怒って話したけれど
温もりは残っていない
朝起きて、目を開けてみると
彼はもういない

手を伸ばしても
もう彼に触れることは出来ない

$$2003.3.10$$

Though We Were Very Close to One Another

Though we were very close to one another,
The distance, which I can reach
If I stretch out my hand, may have changed
Into being a different space from the middle.
A dream in which I wish I could see him everyday
Was just imagined before my eyes.
His warmth is no longer there,
Although it is certain that we talked to each other
With laughter, with anger.
When I woke up and open my eyes
In the morning, he was no longer there.
Even if I reach out my hand,
I can't touch him anymore.

10 March 2003

夢の7日間

さようなら　オーストラリア
さようなら　ブリスベン
また来るからね

白い雪の山を越えて
広い雪の大地を越えて
羊の群れを飛び越えて
また来るからね

待っててね
アンジー、ドンキー、チェロキー
また　いつか会える日まで

2003.5.4

370

Seven Dreamy Days

Goodbye, Australia.
So long, Brisbane.
I'll come back again!
I'll climb over white snow mountains,
Walk over wide snowy ground,
Jump with a flock of sheep, and
Come back again.
Please wait for me,
Angie, Donkey, Cherokee,
Until we can see each other again someday.

4 May 2003

スリランカのヤモリ

ヤモリはじっとして何を考えているのかな
銀歯が取れて、どうしようと不安になったり
沢山虫が飛んで来て、うんざりしたり
スクライルがカカカと鳴いて
怖い思いをしたりするのかな

もし、私がヤモリなら
沢山の虫はご馳走で
壁に這いつくばって、ひっそりと
人間に見つからないように
柱の陰に身を隠すだけ

2003.6.24

A Gecko in Sri Lanka

I wonder what a gecko is thinking
Without moving.
I also wonder if the gecko can be scared
By a squirrel that cries: ka ka ka
Or annoyed by many flying insects
Or become anxious about the solution of
A silver tooth that came out.
If I was the gecko,
Many insects would be my feast and
I would only hide myself behind a pillar
Sticking out of the wall, quietly,
So as not to be found by humans.

24 June 2003

人間って・・・

人は楽しいことより
辛いことをより覚えているという
辛いことがあるたび
辛いことを思い出すたび
自分はどうして生きているのだろうと思う
これらの出来事は自分にとって
何か意味があるのだろうかと思う

大人になるため
成長するため

人は何のために成長するのだろうか
何のために生まれて
何のために生きるのか
時々　その答えが無性に欲しくなる

銃弾を目の前にした時
きっと自分は"生きたい"と思う
大きな病気を告げられた時
きっと"生きたい"と思うのだろう

生きる意味さえも分からないのに
生きたいなんて
人はよく分からない生き物だ

２００３．７．２１

374

Humans Are...

I hear that people remember painful events
More than happy times,
Each time when bitter things happen, and
Each time which I remember hard things,
I consider why I stay alive.
I wonder if these incidents give something
Meaningful to me.
To be an adult?
To grow up?
Why do people have to grow up?
Sometimes I don't know
Why we are born and why we live.
If I faced bullets
I'd certainly think: "I want to stay alive."
If I was told that I had a serious illness,
I'd surely hope to stay alive.
Humans are incomprehensible creatures
Because they hope to stay alive
Although they don't even know the meaning of living.

21 July 2003

ディズニー

電車は４つの駅をグルグル回り
人の夢を乗せて
人の笑顔を乗せて走る

それがディズニー
夢の異空間
人のときめきを乗せて
時折　ちょっと切ない思い出を乗せて
電車は今日も走る

２００３.7.21

DISNEY

A train goes round and round the four stations.
It runs with peoples' dreams and smiles.
It's Disney, a dream-like space that is
Different from this world.
Today the train runs again with peoples' excitement
And sometimes with little melancholy memories.

21 July 2003

ヤドカリの唄

私は　ビール飲みません
タバコも吸いません
ちょっと弱っている私に
構わないで下さい
ちょっと弱っている私に
仲間のヤドカリが声を掛けます

どうせ死ぬなら、その殻をくれ

あぁ　無情
星砂の海はサバイバル
結構　大変です

2003.9.13

378

A Hermit Crab's Song

I don't drink beer.
I also don't smoke cigarettes.
Please leave me alone because I'm a little bit weak.
My hermit crab fellows talk to me,
Who has weakened a little.
"Give me your shell if you die, please."
Oh, how cold-hearted!
The beach of Hoshisuna is survival.
It's tougher to live here, tougher than
You think it is.

13 September 2003

秋の夜の独り言　パート2

幸せを保障するなんて
何ておこがましいことを
思っていたのだろう

幸せにするどころか
あの子は苦しんで
死んでいった
寒いなぁと体を硬直させて
死んでいった

私の心に
この布団のような温かさが
少しでもあったなら
あの子は死なずに済んだ

後悔は秋の夜をさまよう

2003.9.21

A Thought one Autumn Night,
PART TWO

How presumptuous,
I, who wanted to guard your happiness, was.
I didn't make my boy happy
But made him suffer and die.
He passed away freezing,
His body rigid.
If I had had even a little warmth,
Like this futon, in my heart,
My boy would have remained alive.
My regret wanders autumn nights.

21 September 2003

この地球上で

この地球上で
一瞬のうちに生まれて
一瞬のうちに消えていく命

それは　まるで
プクッと生まれて
パチンッと浮かんでは消える
泡のよう

消えた命は何処へ行くのだろう
叩かれて、潰された
蚊の魂は何処へ
浮かんで行くのだろう

そして　また　私の一生も
そんな泡のようなものかも知れないな

地球は回り
風が吹くよ
この地球上で
また新しい命が生まれ
パチンッと音をたてて
消えていくよ

2003.12.10

ON THE EARTH

Lives which appear and disappear
In an instant on the earth.
They are like bubbles that appear, puku
And disappear, pachin.
I wonder where the life that disappears goes to.
I wonder where the spirit of a mosquito
That was crushed by a blow is floating to.
And my whole life may also be like such bubbles.
The earth rotates and the wind blows!
New lives appear and disappear,
Making a sound, pachin again
On the earth.

10 December 2003

人生という名のゲーム

ルール1

頑張ったり、疲れたり、
自分で選択することが出来る

楽をしたり、止まったり、
勿論、一回休んだり、
時には振り出しに戻ったり

人生は自分で決めることが出来る
大きなゲーム
気楽に楽しくやりましょう！

２００４.２.３

A Game, Which We Call Our Life

Rule number 1:
We can choose to do our best.
We can choose to work ourselves to the bone.
We can decide on the course of our life by ourselves:
To be lazy, to stop.
And, of course, to take a rest once in a while.
At times to return to the start, et cetera.
It's such a big game that
We should take it easy and enjoy playing!

3 February 2004

日本を離れる時

春には桜が咲き
夏には蝉の音
秋には鈴虫
冬には雪が舞い
そう、ここは日本

大好きな人の笑顔が
沢山あるここを離れて
私は一体　何を求めているのでしょう

究極の幸せって
一体何なのでしょうね

分からない、分からない
うっすらと遠くに見える光
その先に何があるのか
ただ、知りたいだけなんです

　　　　　　　　　２００４.３.３０

WHEN I LEAVE JAPAN

Cherry blossom trees bloom in spring.
Songs of cicadas in summer.
Bell-ringing crickets in autumn.
Snow dances in winter.
Yes, here is Japan.
I'll leave here, where there are the many smiles
Of the people who I love.
Where on earth will I go?
Father, Mother,
What in the world am I asking for?
What is the supreme happiness?
I don't know, I don't know.
I just simply want to know
What is there ahead of the faint light
Which I can see far away.

30 March 2004

だんご虫

だんご虫よ
勝手に私の部屋に入って来て
ひっくり返り、勝手に死んでゆく
例え、元に戻れたとしても
私の靴が君を襲うだろう

君の亡骸は
蜘蛛様が来て食べてしまうだろう
その蜘蛛様も
噴射にあって、殺される運命にある

いくつもの生命が失われ、
わずかな光が別れを歌う
ここは何て悲しい墓場なのだろう

２００４.７.４

Dango-mushi (Burestids)

Dango-mushi,
You enter my room without permission
And then turn over and die at your convenience.
Even though you can return to your original position,
My shoe will attack you.
Spiders will come and eat your dead body.
The spiders are also doomed to be killed
By jets of spray.
Many lives disappear and
Trifling sunlight sings a lamentation for the farewell.
What a sad graveyard this place is.

4 July 2004

ある晴天の日の日記

今日は晴れです
青い空を見たら、悲しくなりました
夏の終わりを感じたからかも知れません
最近、あまり良くなかったから
最後に良いところを見せようと思ったのかな
本当に綺麗な青い空なので
泣きたくなりました

2004.7.18

DAIRY OF A LOVELY DAY

It's a sunny day today.
When I saw the blue sky I felt sad.
It may have been because
I had felt the end of summer.
I wonder if the sky wanted to show
The best at the end
Because the weather hadn't been so nice recently.
It was such a beautiful blue sky that
I felt like crying.

18 July 2004

Ｄｅａｒ　Ｆｒｉｅｎｄ

君がいなくなっても
地球は回る
君がいなくなっても
朝は来る
草木が枯れてしまっても
春が来れば
また実を付け、花が咲く

だけど、私は悲しいよ
君がいなくなったら
このアイルランドの空のように
私の心も曇ってしまうだろう
太陽を失った花がしおれてしまうように
私もまたしおれてしまうだろう

２００４.７.２６

DEAR FRIEND

Even though you leave,
The earth will continue to go round.
Even though you won't be here,
Morning will come.
Even though a branch withers,
The tree will bud and bloom
After the arrival of spring.
However, I am sad
If you are not here,
My heart will also be cloudy,
Like this Irish sky.
I will also languish
As flowers languish without the sun.

26 July 2004

たんぽぽの綿毛

たんぽぽの綿毛が迷い込んで来た
綿毛はあの飛行機のように
空高く飛べるのかも知れない
バスの中に迷い込んで
フッと息で吹き飛ばされるのかも知れない

今日、日本へ戻らなければならない
友よ
私達の人生なんて
そんなものかも知れないよ

2004.8.2

DOWN OF DANDELIONS

Down of a dandelion strayed.
The down may be able to fly high
Like an airplane in the sky.
It may stray into a bus and
Be blown by a breath: fu!
My friend, who has to go back to Japan today,
Our life, so-called, may be similar to such a thing.

2 August 2004

空虚な空の下

空にポッカリと穴が開いてしまった
それだけ　あなたの存在が大きかった
ということなのだろう

でも、その穴はすぐに埋まる
そう遠くないうちに埋まることを
知っている
それが人間の生きる力なのだ
と信じている
傷はいつの間にか治り、
暗い心もまた　いつの間にか
癒されているものなのだ

2004.8.30

396

Under the Empty Sky

A hole appeared in the sky: pokkari.
I think it means that your existence was
Extremely significant for me.
Yet, the hole will be fixed.
I know that it will be buried before long.
I believe that it is in a human's power to live.
Wounds will heal before we know it, and
Cloudy hearts will be mended as well
Before we know it.

30 August 2004

Ｓｔａｒｇａｚｅ

友よ
この星空を見上げてごらん

沢山星があるでしょう
この銀河の宇宙の中では
私達の存在はちっぽけな存在
私達の周りで起こる出来事は
本当に小さな出来事

だから、そんなことで
死ぬなんて言っちゃだめだよ
君の命はこの大宇宙の中で
たった一つの尊い存在

もし、死んでしまったら
この星空はもう見られないよ
本当に大切な物を見つけてからでも
遅くはないよ
みんな　いつかは消えてなくなるのだから

この星空を見上げて、美しいと思えることが
どんなに素晴らしいことか
君には分かるだろうか

2004.9.9

STARGAZE

My dear friend,
Look up at the starry sky!
There are many stars, aren't there?
Our existences are tiny existences
In the galaxy.
The events, which happen around us, are
Really tiny incidents.
So, you shouldn't say that you will die
Because of such things.
Your life is the only one and
A precious existence in this great universe.
If you die,
You won't be able to look at this starry sky anymore.
It's not too late
Even though it is after you find
The really important things.
Because we all disappear and
Won't exist in this world someday.
I hope you can understand
What a wonderful thing it is
That you can feel it beautiful
When you look at this starry sky.

9 September 2004

太陽の光と幸せ

人は太陽の光の中にいるとき
それを当たり前と思う
夜が来て、朝が来るのは
当然と思っている

太陽の光が無くなったとき
人は
あの時、自分は幸せだったのだと気付く

どんな状況でも
決して最悪ではないのだと思っている人は
果たして
どのくらいいるのだろうか

2005.2.13

SUNLIGHT AND HAPPINESS

When we are in sunlight,
We feel that it is natural.
We are thinking it is natural that
Morning should come after night.
When we lost the sunlight,
We realized that
We had been happy at the time when the sun shown.
How many people are thinking that
It's not the worst
No matter what the situation is?

13 February 2005

チョコレート

チョコレートは私の精神安定剤
不安をかき消してくれる
無くなると無性に欲しくなる
麻薬のようなもの

もし　私がとても太ったら
あなたのせいよ
と、人のせいにしながら
またひとかじり・・・

だって　この瞬間は本当に幸せなんだもの
2005.6.19

CHOCOLATE

Chocolate is my tranquilizer.
It's helpful in vanishing my worries.
If I run out of it
I really want chocolate.
It's like a drug.
One more bite, blaming chocolate:
"It's your fault
If I gain weight!"
Because I am really happy
At this moment.

19 June 2005

ロールシャッハ
―風呂場の金具が物語ること―

白い人が泣いている
黒い人が泣いている
　皆　大変なんだね
　皆　大変でも幸せならいいね
明日はどんな日になるかな
　皆　頑張ろうね

白い人が笑っている
黒い人が笑っている
ささやかな幸せでも
笑えるならいいね
明日もまた笑えるかな
　皆　頑張ろうね

明日はどんな顔に見えるかな

2005.6.19

RORSCHACH

(things that the metal fittings in my bathroom tell)

A white-faced person is crying.
A black-faced person is crying.
It is tough on everybody.
Even though we have a hard life,
If we are happy,
It's okay, isn't it?
I wonder how it will be tomorrow.
Cheer up, everybody!
A white-faced person is smiling.
A black-faced person is smiling.
Even though it is a modest happiness,
If we can smile,
It's okay, isn't it?
I wonder if we can smile tomorrow as well.
Cheer up, everybody!
How will their faces look tomorrow?

19 June 2005

素敵な一日になりますように

ベッドの上で横になっている時
とても清々しい青空の日
イチゴ畑で昼寝をしているように感じたら
それはきっと幸せな証拠

今日一日がとても素晴らしかったと感じたら
それは本当に幸せな証拠

あの時私は幸せだったと感じたら
多かれ少なかれ
生活を変える必要があります

あなたのアドバイザーはあなた
あなたをよく知っているのは
あなたなのだから
自分で自分を幸せに導いて

2005.6.19

I Wish You a Wonderful Day

When you are lying on the bed,
If you feel as if you were taking a nap
In a strawberry field on a day of
Very clear blue skies,
It is a proof that you're happy.
If you feel that today was very wonderful,
It is certainly a proof that you're happy.
If you feel that you were happy at that time,
You need to change your lifestyle
More or less.
You are your own advisor.
You are the person who knows yourself well.
So, lead yourself to your own happiness.

19 June 2005

夏の空

夏の空は大きい

雲よ
私を何処か連れて行って
何処か楽しい気分になる所へ
何処か素敵な風が吹く所へ

風よ
私の願いを聞いておくれ
どうか　私の気持ちを伝えてね
どうか　いつもハッピーでいられますように
と、日本のみんなに伝えてね

風に乗って、雲に乗って
旅をしたい
夏の空は大きい

２００５.７.１６

Summer Sky

The summer sky is immense.
Clouds,
Please take me somewhere.
Somewhere where I can feel happy.
Somewhere where a wonderful wind blows.
Wind,
Could you please do me a favour?
Please tell them my feelings.
Please tell all in Japan that
I wish them happiness all the time.
I would like to travel by
Wind and cloud.
The summer sky is immense.

16 July 2005

自然の芸術
―キャッシェル行きのバスの中にて―

空に広がる白い雲
なんて壮大でゴージャスなんだろう
空にポッカリと浮かぶ白い月
その下で緑の木々が揺れている

なんて綺麗な水色なんだろう
なんで雲は白いのか
なんて素敵な色のコントラスト
なんで自然の芸術は
こんなに　こんなに
素晴らしいのか！

神様がくれた贈り物
自然の芸術
人は作ることが出来ないね

2005.9.25

Natural Art

(on a bus to Cashel)

White clouds expand in the sky.
How magnificent and gorgeous it is!
A white moon in the sky: pokkari.
Green trees are swaying under the moon.
What a beautiful light blue it is!
Why are clouds white?
What fabulous and contrasting colours they are!
Why is natural art so wonderful like this?
A gift God gave us.
Natural art,
We can't create it, can we?

25 September 2005

泣いて帰った帰り道

蝸牛を踏んだ
蝸牛は死んだ

道が暗かったし、
泣いていたから、分からなかったの

蝸牛は言った
どんなにショックで辛くても
死ぬわけじゃないから
大丈夫だよ

蝸牛は逝った
私は生きている
蝸牛は身をもって教えてくれたんだね

2005.9.30

I Returned Home Crying

I stepped on a snail.
The snail died.
I didn't see you
Because the street was dark and
I was crying.
The snail said:
"Don't worry because you won't die
No matter how much you are shocked
And disappointed."
The snail passed away.
I am still alive.
He taught me through his death.

30 September 2005

太陽の下で

人は皆
平和な幸せを願っているのに
どうして戦争は無くならないの
いつになったら
争いや憎しみ合いは終わるの

暴力は人の心をも傷つけるね
爆発は一瞬で
多くの大切な物を奪うよね
それがあなたには分からないの

悲しいね
そんな世界に住む私達
それが人間の性ならば

2006.2.9

UNDER THE SUN

Though we all wish for peaceful happiness,
Why doesn't war disappear?
When will battles and hatred be over?
Violence hurts out hearts as well,
Doesn't it?
Explosions deprive many valuable things
In an instant.
Don't you understand that?
Sorrowful.
We who live in such a world.
If it is human nature.

9 February 2006

治療法

痛みに弱い私は
嫌なことを忘れるように
水中に潜って
ひたすら
眠る　眠る　眠る・・・

いっそ　このまま死んでしまえたら
と思ってみても
それは出来ない
大好きなあなたに会えなくなってしまうから
大好きなあなたに会うことを夢見て
ひたすら
眠る　眠る　眠る・・・

素敵な明日を夢見て
眠る　眠る　眠る・・・

2006.2.27

CURE

I who am vulnerable to pains
Sleep, sleep, sleep entirely
Under the water
In order to forget things which bother me.
I can't do so,
Even though I think that
It would be nice if I died
In this situation now.
Because I wouldn't be able to see
You, who I really love.
I sleep, sleep, sleep,
Dreaming of a wonderful tomorrow.

27 February 2006

雨宿りしながら

雨宿りしながら
私の人生って何なんだと思った

礼儀正しくしなくちゃと
人に気を遣ったり
自分の夢だからと
疲れていても頑張ったり
時々　私って
馬鹿みたいと思ってしまうけど
これが自分の人生なんだからいいんだ
と考え直してみたり・・・

疲れる人生を送るのは
みんな自分のせいだと思う
でも、だからといって
そんな急には変えられないよ
自分の道は自分で選ぶし
自分の道は自分で歩くのだから

こんな人生を歩むのは
こんな自分のせい
だから　仕方ないよ

2006.4.18

While I was Taking Shelter from the Rain

When I was taking shelter from the rain,
I thought about what the meaning of life was.
I sometimes feel stupid
Because I pay attention to others,
To be courteous and
Push myself hard, even though I am tired.
But I consider that it's okay
Because it is my life.
I think it's because of myself
That I have a hard life.
However, I can't change myself all of a sudden.
It's because of myself
That I have such a life
As I choose my own path and
I walk on the way I choose.
So there is nothing to do for it.

18 April 2006

エレジー

何故生きるのかも分からないけど
死んでしまったら
このパンの残りを食べることすら出来ない
大好きなあの人に会うことも
一緒に笑うことも出来ない

誰にでも最後は訪れる
それは突然かも知れない
誰も知らない間に
ひっそりと起こるのかも知れない

だから　毎日楽しく
一生懸命生きなくてはいけない
相手にも優しくしてあげた方がいいね

明日の朝　このパンの残りを食べよう
また大好きなあの人に会って
一緒に笑おう

　　　　　　　　　　　２００６.６.２６

ELEGY

I couldn't even eat the rest of this bread
If I died,
Although I don't know why I keep on living.
I couldn't see the person, who I really love,
And we couldn't laugh together.
The end will visit everybody.
It may be all of a sudden.
It may happen silently
Before you know it.
Therefore, we have to live happily,
Thriving everyday.
It's better to be lenient with others.
I'll eat the rest of this bread tomorrow morning.
I'll see my beloved person and we will
Laugh together again.

26 June 2006

秋の木漏れ日

小さな世界の中で
私達は幸せだった
喧嘩をしたりして
例え、嫌だと思うことがあっても
それは小さな世界の小さな出来事
（その当時からすれば、
　重大な事件だったのだけれど）
少なくとも
私は幸せだった
いつも幸せだった

もう一度生まれ変わるとしても
私はまた私に生まれたい

今度はもっと色々な事を注意して見て
困っている時は助けてあげて
家族をもっと大切にしてあげよう

2006.9.17

422

Autumn Sunlight Through The Trees

We were happy in a small world.
Even though we disliked each other during arguments,
They were tiny incidents in a small world.
(They seemed like very important incidents at the time.)
At least I was happy.
We were always together.
If I had a chance to be born once again,
I would like to be myself again.
I would observe many things carefully
And help them when they were in trouble
And take care of my family more
Next time.

17 September 2006

幸せなどんぐり

公園を急いで歩いている時
どんぐりが私の肩を叩いた

「そんなに急ぐなよ！
　景色がこんなに綺麗じゃないか。
　もっと　人生を楽しめよ！
　気付いていない素晴らしい物が
　まだ沢山あるじゃないか。」

疲れて家路に辿り着いた時
小さなどんぐりが
ひょっこり顔を出して、言った

「お疲れ様、
　もう　ゆっくり休んでいいんだよ。」

「ありがとう。
　君のお陰で、幸せな気分になったよ。」
　　　　　　　　　　２００６．１０．２６

424

Happy Acorn

When I was walking quickly in a park,
An acorn tapped my shoulder.
"Don't hurry like that!
The scenery is so beautiful here, isn't it?
Enjoy your life more!
There are many wonderful things that
You haven't noticed yet!"
When I became tired and returned home,
The little acorn turned up unexpectedly and said:
"Hard work!
You can take your time and relax now!"
"Yes, thank you. I became happy, thanks to you."

26 October 2006

Everything
will be alright

今　気が付いた
私は小さい頃から
安心して眠ったことがない
いつも何かしら
心配事をしていたような気がする

大丈夫だよ
何とかなるよ
という　何の根拠もない
ただの慰めは嫌いだが

everything
will be alright
という幻のような声を聞いて
涙するのは
年を取ったからだろうか

everything is going
to be all right
という陽気な言葉に
妙に反応して
心地良さを感じるのは
何故だろうか

2006.12.2

426

Everything Will be Alright

Now I realize.
I have never slept with relief
Since I was a child.
I feel that I had worried about something
All the time.
I hate mere consolation without a basis
Such as, "It's okay, things will work out."
But is it because I became old that
I shed tears when I heard a voice like
An illusion: "Everything will be alright"?
Why do I strangely react to a merry word:
"Everything is going to be alright."
And why do I feel comfortable?

2 December 2006

お月様との約束

どしゃ降りの雲が去った後
小さいけれど、くっきりとしたお月様が
顔を出して言った

「嫌なことがあっても、くじけるでないぞ。
　大変なことがあっても、決して諦めることなく、
　頑張り続けるのだ。
　それだけが、お前に出来ることなのだから。」

「はい。分かりました。そうします。」

もう一度見上げてお月様を見たが、
お月様はもう何も言わず、
澄んだ星空に浮かんで
ただ輝くだけだった

2007.1.4

428

A Promise with the Moon

After the heavy rain clouds left,
The moon, which was small, but sharp,
Turned up and said:
"Hang in there,
Even though something annoys you.
Never give up, and keep making an effort,
Even though there are things that are difficult for you
Because it's all you can do."
"Yes, alright. I'll do so."
I looked up at the moon once again,
But the moon didn't say anything more
And just sparked, floating in the clear starry sky.

4 January 2007

この風が地球を廻るとき

この風に乗って
強い風の日
彼女は旅立って行った
空港へ行く途中
ジャンプ！！
この風に乗って
飛んで行きなさい
急いで、急いで！
背中を押された

フライトアテンダントの
コートがヒラヒラ

バスドライバーの
煙草もビュービュー
私は神様が言った通りに
本当に風に乗って
ジャンプして空港へ行ったんだよ
本当だよ

この風が地球を廻るとき
また会おうね

2007.1.18

430

WHEN THE WIND BLOWS AROUND THE EARTH

On a very windy day
She climbed onto the wind and started off.
I jumped to the airport.
"Go on this wind and fly to the airport.
Hurry up! Hurry up!"
My back was pushed.
A flight attendant's coat was pulled off:
Hira hira.
A bus driver's cigarette was also blown:
Byuu byuu.
Honestly, I climbed onto the wind and jumped
To the airport, as God said to do.
It's true.
When this wind blows around the earth again,
Shall we again meet?

18 January 2007

アイルランドのアゲハ蝶

黒いアゲハ蝶が勢いよく飛び込んで来て言った

やめた！やめた！
疲れているなら
バスの中で仕事することないよ
お腹が痛いなら
ルアスに乗ってまで仕事することないよ
さあ、やめた！やめた！

私は教師
疲れていても　頑張らなくてはいけないの
例え　病気でも
疲れている生徒を励まし、エナジーを与え、
例え　自分が不幸でも
生徒の幸せを願うのよ
私は教師になる為に生まれてきたの
私に出来ることは
ただ頑張ることだけ・・・

あぁ、あぁ、それなら好きにおしよ
折角忠告してやってるのに
日本人はこれだから、まったく！
じゃ、さようなら
仕事中毒の日本人さん！

そう言って　プイッと後ろを向くと
アゲハ蝶は黒い葉っぱになってしまった
その葉っぱを手に取って眺めている私に
隣に座っている人が言った

強い風で葉っぱが飛んで来たんだね

えぇ、とてもびっくりしたわ

とてもね
　　　　　　　　　2007.1.19

A Swallowtail in Ireland

A black swallowtail rushed into a Luas tram
With great momentum and said:
"Stop, stop!
If you are tired, you shouldn't work on a bus.
If you have a stomachache,
You don't have to work on a Luas tram.
Come on, stop, stop!!"
"I'm a teacher.
I have to do my best, even though I'm tired.
I encourage and give energy to
My students who are tired
Even if I am sick myself.
I wish my students happiness
Even if I'm unhappy.
I was born to be a teacher.
All I can do is to make an effort."
"Okay, okay, then do as you like.
I gave you advice,
Yet, the Japanese are always like this.
Whew..."

Then, so long, Japanese workaholic!"
The swallowtail turned into a black leaf
After it had said this and turned around quickly: *pui.*
A person who was sitting next to me said:
"The leaf was blown inside
By a strong wind, wasn't it?"
"Yes, I was very surprised. Really..."

19 January 2007

時の止まった運河

運河に浮かんで
空を眺めていれば
いつも一緒にいる二羽の白鳥が近付いてきて
語り掛ける

お疲れですか
時の止まった運河へようこそ
ここには毎日の疲労やストレス
悩みもありません
ちょっとしたリラクゼーションスパに
なっております
どうぞ　ごゆっくりなさっていって下さいませ

その声はなんと美しく
物腰はなんと荘厳あふれ
優美なことか！！

その後で　ぜんまい仕掛けの
玩具のような緑の顔をした鴨が
御用は何なりと　お申しつけ下さいませ！

と、元気よく言って
白鳥の後をついて行った

そうだ！
今　私に必要なのは
これなのだ！！

2007.6.6

A TIMELESS CANAL

If I am viewing the sky,
Floating on the canal
Two swans that are always together
Come closely and talk to me:
"Are you tired?
Welcome to a timeless canal.
There is no daily tiredness, stress,
Or problems here.
Here is a kind of relaxation spa.
Please enjoy and relax."
What a beautiful voice!
How superb and graceful their demeanor is!

After that a duck that has a green face like a spring toy said:
"Please let me know without hesitation
If you possess something!"
And then he followed the swans.
Yes, that's what I need now!!

6 June 2007

Ｄｅｒｒｙの叫び

Ｄｅｒｒｙの人は悲しみと共に生きている
いつになったら
本当の幸せを取り戻すことが出来るのだろうか

何故
このｌａｎｄとｓｐｉｒｉｔｓは
Ｉｒｉｓｈだと言わないのか

笑っていても本当に笑っていない
Ｄｅｒｒｙの悲劇は今でも続いている

終わらない悲劇
それが悲劇

何故
みんな気付かないのか
それとも目を瞑っているの
聞かないように耳をふさいでいるの
Ｄｅｒｒｙの叫び

２００７.９.８

SCREAM OF DERRY

The people of Derry have lived with sorrow.
When will they be able to regain
True happiness?
Why don't they insist that
This land and its spirit are Irish?
They are not smiling from the bottom of their hearts
Even though they seem to be smiling.
Tragedy in Derry has continued still.
Endless tragedy.
It is their tragedy.
Why can't people realize it?
Or are they just shutting their eyes?
Are they covering their ears
So that they don't hear?
Scream of Derry.

8 September 2007

蜘蛛様と蛾

頭上に蜘蛛様がいる
どうやったら出て行ってもらえるかと
見つめながら考えていたら
何処かに行ってしまった

光を求めて蛾がやって来た
蜘蛛様がつたって行った
天井の糸が揺れている

どちらが得か、よく考えろと言っている

私は無闇な殺生はしたくありません
分かりました
では、蜘蛛様
どうぞ宜しくお願い致します
と、偽善者の私が言った

2007.9.8

MISTER SPIDER AND A MOTH

Mister Spider was overheard.
While I was thinking
How I could succeed in making him leave,
He went somewhere.
A moth came over for the light.
A thread on the ceiling that
Mister Spider used to travel on was wavering.
It was telling me to consider
Which was profitable to me.
I who am hypocritical said:
"I wouldn't like to kill indiscriminately.
Alright, then,
I'll leave it to you, Mister Spider."

8 September 2007

アイルランドに戻る飛行機の中で

鳥になって
今すぐ日本へ帰りたい
この行く先に何があるのか

だんだん小さくなる
見送りで手を振る母の姿を
あと何回　見ることが出来るのだろう

甘えて頼む娘の声に
張り切る父

気を遣ってくれている姉夫婦
懐いてくれている姪っ子達

いつも空港まで来てくれる姉
胸が締め付けられる思いで下る
エスカレーター

日本とアイルランドが
隣同士だったら良かったのに

国へ帰る人
旅行をする人
楽しい笑顔の中
私は一人　思う

2008.1.5

444

ON AN AIRPLANE TO RETURN TO IRELAND

I'd like to become a bird and
Go back to Japan immediately.
What is there ahead going in this direction?
How many times can I see my Mother waving her hands
To see me off and getting smaller little by little?
My Father, who works hard for the requests
Of his daughters, who depend on him.
My older sister and her husband, who care about me.
My nieces, who are attached to me.
My older sister, who always comes to the airport with me.
An escalator that I descend with my feelings of distress.
I wish Japan and Ireland were neighbors.
People who return to their country.
People who go traveling.
I think these thoughts, alone in the atmosphere of
Happy smiles.

5 January 2008

前を向いて歩こう

いつも前を向いて
元気に歩こう
でも、ちょっと疲れたり、辛い時は
立ち止まって、後ろを振り返ってごらん

そこには　夢の入り口
何も分からなくて
不安と戸惑いの中にいる
自分がいるよ

もう一度振り返ったら
そこには
夢を追いかけて、頑張っている自分と
夢を早く叶えたくて、もどかしい気持ちでいる
自分がいるよ

今、時のレールの上に
今の私がいる
夢の途中

未来の私は今の私を
どんな風に思うのかな

私はまた前を向いて
元気に歩くだけです

2008.1.15

446

Let's Walk, Looking Forward

Let's walk cheerfully, looking forward most of the time.
But sometimes pausing to look back
When we are tired and going through a hard time.
You will be there at the entrance of your dreams.
You, who are anxious and confused
Because you know nothing, will be there.
If you look back once more,
You, who are trying hard to follow your dreams, and
You, who are feeling frustrated
Because you want to make your dream
Come true quickly, will be there.
Currently I of the present am traveling on time's railway.
On my way to my dreams.
I wonder what the future I will think about the present me.
I just walk cheerfully, looking ahead.

15 January 2008

死刑の椅子

これは牢屋の臭い
ここには誰もいない
ただ、死刑の椅子があるだけ
あの楽しくて、眩しい日々は
何処へ行ってしまったのか

みんな　いなくなってしまう
一人、また一人
私から離れてゆく
そして、また一人
今、また一人
私の夢や希望は薄く霞んでゆき
暗い闇の中へ消えてゆく

それは死刑判決に似ている

私はこの椅子に座って
孤独に死んでゆくのか
この薄暗い牢屋の中で
懐かしい昔を振り返りながら
死んでゆけば良いのか

時計はカチカチと音をたてて
私の死を急き立てているようだ

私に時間を下さい
また一から頑張りますから
私に希望を下さい

生きる希望
もっと強く生きる勇気
悲しみを乗り越える強さ
未来をこの手で創るために
幸せな未来があるように

２００８.３.２２

A Chair for the Death Penalty

This is the smell of a prison.
Nobody is here.
There is just a chair for the death penalty.
Where did the merry and brilliant days go?
All will disappear.
One after another.
They are leaving me.
Moreover, one after another again.
My dreams and hopes are paling and
Will fade out into gloomy darkness.
It is similar to the death penalty.
Am I going to die in solitude,
Sitting on this chair?
Should I die reminiscing about my good old days
In this dim jail?
A clock seems to hurry me into death,
Making a sound: kachi kachi.
Please give me more time,
As I will try again from the beginning.

Please give me hope.
The hope to live.
The courage to live more strongly.
The strength to get over sorrow.
In order to make my future by myself.
For my happy future.

22 March 2008

Merrion Squareにて

小鳥が近寄って来て、言った
「こんにちは。それ、おいしそうですね。」
「はい、おいしいですよ。」

小鳥は何も言わなかったが、
目で訴えた
「それ、下さい。それ、私に下さい！！」
私がパンを小さくちぎってあげると
小鳥はそれを拾って、
サッと飛んで行ってしまった

「ありがとう。」
と、言ったかどうかは定かではないが、
多分、言ったと思う

次に蠅が近寄って来た
蜂もすぐそこまで来た
「だめ、だめ！もう、あげないよ！」
彼らも飛んで行った

風が吹いて、木々が揺れる
虫達は木の周りで遊ぶ
木の葉は輪を描いて踊る
自然が私に語り掛けている

2008.6.6

In Merrion Square

A little bird came closer and said:
"Hello, that looks delicious!"
"Yes, it is delicious."
The little bird didn't say anything else,
But he appealed to me with his eyes:
"Give me that! Give me that, please!!"
I gave him a piece of bread that I had crumbled up.
He picked it up and flew away quickly.
"Thank you."
I am not sure if he said so or not,
But I think that he said so maybe.
Next a fly approached me.
A bee also came just there.
"No, no!
I won't give you any more of my bread!"
They flew away too.
Wind blows and trees sway.
Insects play around the trees.
Leaves dance, drawing a circle.
Nature is talking to me.

6 June 2008

タイムスリップ

あれ、そこに置いてあった物が無くなっている
そこにいた人もいない

そうか、時空を飛び越えて、
ここに引っ越す前に戻って来たのだ

どうするのが一番良いのか
あの時どうすれば良かったのか
幸せな未来へ自分を導く為には
今、どうすべきなのか

過去に戻って来て、
やり直せるチャンスがある今も
未だ答えは見つからない
答えは頭の中の
深い霧に包まれている
それが人生というものなのか

2008.10.12

TIME JUMP

Oh, objects that once were here disappeared.
People who were once here also vanished away.
I see....
I returned to the time before I had moved here
By jumping through time and space.
What is the best thing to do?
What should I have done in those days?
What should I do now
To lead myself to my happy future?
I haven't found the answers yet
In spite of the chance to return to my past and try again.
The answers have been wrapped
In a deep mist in my mind.
Is that our life?

12 October 2008

Ｄｉｎｇｌｅ　Ｂａｙの巨人

Ｄｉｎｇｌｅ　Ｂａｙに浮かびながら
いつも昼寝をしている巨人がいます。

夜、暗くなって、街の灯りが消えてから
巨人は起きて、陸に上がって来ます。

いくつもの畑を
のっし、のっし、跨いで
あるＢ＆Ｂに来ました。
そして、窓を覗き込んで言いました。

明日がどうなるか、なんて分からない。
ただ、幸せな明日を迎える為に、
今日、一生懸命頑張るだけさ。
人の人生は辛くも、簡単にもなる。
それを選ぶのは自分。
一度、それを選んだら、
毎日が楽しいと思えるように
自分を導かなければならない。
また、それが出来なくても
がっかりすることはないんだよ。
また頑張れば良いのだから。

そう言って、海に帰って行きました。
                                    ２００８.１０.２７

A GIANT IN DINGLE BAY

There is a giant who always takes a nap
Floating in Dingle Bay.
He gets up and comes to the land
After it becomes dark and
The lights in the town go off at night.
He strode over patches of land: nosshi nosshi
And came to a B&B.
Next he looked inside a window and said:
We don't know what will happen tomorrow.
We should just work hard today
To welcome happiness tomorrow.
Our life can be both hard and easy.
It's you who makes the choice.
Once you make your choice
You have to lead yourself
To be able to feel happy everyday.
Also, you don't have to be disappointed
Even if you can't do so.
Because there won't be a problem if you try again.
He said this and went back to the ocean.

27 October 2008

猫の独り言

にこは猫
猫は猫なりに時を過ごす
英語のレッスンに行ったり
日本語のレッスンに行ったり
掃除をしたり
洗濯をしたり
買い物をしたり
遊んだり

今年はあっという間だったニャー
と満足気に笑みを漏らし

いくら波乱万丈でも
最後に良かった
幸せだと思えることが大切なのだ
来年も良い年になるといいニャー
と独り言を言った

2008.12.20

458

A Cat's Soliloquy

Niko is a cat.
This cat spends her time living at her own pace.
She goes to English lessons and Japanese lessons,
She cleans her house,
She washes her clothes,
She goes shopping and plays…
She smiles with satisfaction, saying:
"This year has passed very quickly, nyaa."
And she also whispered:
"It's very important for us
To have such an ending that
We can feel happy about
However checkered our life may be.
I hope that we will be happy next year
As well, nyaa."

20 December 2008

おにぎりパワー

笑顔で手を振る空港の姉
思わず　泣きそうになる
泣く代わりに
元気な笑顔で大きく手を振ろう

それぞれの人の
それぞれの人生
皆　一生懸命頑張っている

飛行機の中で　寂しくなったら
このおにぎりを食べよう

行ってきます！

2009.1.10

ONIGIRI POWER

My older sister is waving her hand
With a smile in the airport.
I nearly cry in spite of myself.
I will wave my hand vigorously
With a cheerful smile instead of crying.
Each person has their own way of living.
We all are doing our best.
I will live and do my utmost day after day,
Thinking that everyday is precious,
As they do.
I will have this onigiri
If I feel lonely on an airplane.
Ittekimasu!

10 January 2009

あの時、私はホッとした

正直、あの時　私はホッとした
もう　人の苦しみは見たくなかったからだ
そして、最近　漸く
私はフロイトのようになっていた事に気付く

彼女は彼女なりに頑張っていた
その人がだめな人間って
どうやって決めるの？
尊敬出来る人と　だめな人って
どうやって区別出来るの？

その価値観って　見る角度で
随分　変わるものなんだね
例え　今更でも
それに本当に気付くことが出来たのは
幸いだったと思う

2009.4.17

I WAS RELIEVED AT THE TIME

To be honest, I was relieved at the time
Because I didn't want to see their agony anymore.
And finally, I have recently realized
That I had become like Freud.
She was doing her best in her own way.
How can we judge that a person is valueless?
How can we tell a respectable person
From an unrespectable person?
Our judgment can change
Depending on our point of view, can't it?
I feel that I am so lucky that I realized that
Even though it took until today.

17 April 2009

蘭

わぁ、花が咲いたよ！
今朝まで蕾だったのに、
綺麗だね
素晴らしいね
お花さんも一生懸命生きているんだね
でも、咲く瞬間を見られなかったのは
残念だったな
この花達も　１つ１つ　ポトリと落ちて
いつかは　みんな　いなくなってしまうのだろう
それが定めと知りながら、
この花の美しさと健気さが
妙に儚さを引き立てる
気高く、白い花、蘭。

２００９.５.９

A SAND SHIP

There are two children on the beach.
They talked it over and decided to make a ship out of sand
And float it on the sea.
They were doing their best to make one
But the sand ship continuously broke apart soon
Before they finished making it.
Nevertheless, the sand ship was finished at last.
"We have done it, finally!"
"Here we go! Let's carry it cautiously and float it on the sea!"
They tried to hold it tenderly with their hands.
But the sand ship crumbled in a moment.
They were disappointed and cried.

9 May 2009

蘭・狂い咲き

わぁ、花が咲いたよ。綺麗だね。
"もっと　水をくれ。暑いんだよ。"

花が五つになった。
十一月にもらったけど、長生きするもんだね。
まだ　幾つか蕾があるから、
もっと咲くのかな。楽しみ！
"蕾がある・・・。
太陽の光や水の分け前が少なくなるから、
咲かなくていいよ。"

わぁ、すごい！十番目の花が咲きそうだよ。
それに、まだまだ蕾もある。
みんな　仲良く並んで、本当に綺麗だね。
"おい、おい、押すんじゃねぇよ！"
"そっちこそ、花びら　伸ばしすぎだろ！
もう少し　場所を分けてくれたって
いいじゃねぇか。"
"うるせぇ、今度押したら、お前の花びら
むしり取るぞ、こらっ！"

次の花は、いつ咲くのかな。
楽しみだなぁー。

2009.6.5

466

ORCHID: UNTIMELY FLOWERING

Wow, another flower came out!
How beautiful they are!

"Give me more water. I am thirsty."

Now there are five flowers.
It has a long life, doesn't it?
I received it last November.
I wonder if more flowers will bloom
Because it still has some more buds.
It's exciting!

"There are some buds...
Don't bloom
Because my share of the sunlight and water will become less."

Wow, great!
It seems that the tenth flower will bloom soon.
And also the branch has some more buds.
They are lined up in perfect harmony
And they are so gorgeous, aren't they?

"Hey, hey, don't push me!"
"It's you!
You have stretched your petals too much!"
"Shut up! I'm going to pluck your petals off
If you push me next time, you know?"

I am wondering when the next flower will come out.
I am looking forward to meeting her.

5 June 2009

花と朝焼け

葉の上に　ポトリと落ちた花は
最後の日光浴を楽しむ
葉に映し出されるその影は
何と儚きことか
段々寒くなって、直に冬になる
朝焼けを見つめながら、
この花は、何を物思うのか

２００９.１０.８

468

A Flower and A Morning Glow

A flower which dropped on a leaf is enjoying a last sun bath.
How fragile is the shadow under the leaf.
It is getting cold gradually
And winter will come soon.
What is this flower thinking about
While it is looking at the morning glow.

8 October 2009

愛と危機とソーセージ

危機が起こりました。
その価値が上がりました。
その人は欲を出し、
その危機を利用しようと考えました。
その人はソーセージを五千円で売りました。

他の可能性が出てきました。
その価値が下がりました。
誰も五千円のソーセージは欲しくありません。
それでも、
その人はソーセージを五千円で売り続けました。

結局、その人は
欲とプライドで身を滅ぼしました。

$$2009.10.18$$

Love, a Crisis and a Sausage

A crisis broke out.
The value increased.
The man became greedy and
Tried to take advantage of the crisis.
He sold a sausage for five thousand yen.

Other possibilities appeared.
The value decreased.
Nobody wanted a five thousand yen sausage anymore.
Even so,
He continued trying to sell the sausage for five thousand yen.

Ultimately he damned himself
Because of his greed and pride.

18 October 2009

二人

二人だから出来ること
綺麗で、広くて、暖かい部屋
誰かが帰って来る足音を聞いて、
ワクワクすること
帰って来た時に誰かが「お帰り！」って
言ってくれるのは、いいね
美味しいパンケーキ！
食べながら　お喋りするのは楽しいね

二人だから巻き起こること
喧嘩、いがみ合い、相手を非難すること
ストレス！

一人でいる方がいいと思ったり、
一人でいるより淋しいと感じたり・・・

2009.12.5

Two People

There are things that we can do because we are two.
Clean, wide and warm rooms.
Excitement from hearing the sound of approaching footsteps.
It is very nice to hear "okaeri" when I return home.
Delicious pancakes!
It is really fun to talk about something
While we are eating pancakes.

There are things that happen because we are two.
Fighting, quarreling and criticizing one another.
Stress!

I am thinking that it is better to be alone,
Feeling more lonely than being alone
And so on...

5 December 2009

殺された豚　　—目撃者の証言—

えぇ、私　見たんです。
あの日、豚は
いつものように平穏に生活していました。
男達が連れに来た時も
何の抵抗もなく、すんなり出て行きました。
いつも餌をくれる人達ですから、
慣れたものでした。

腰を付けて、足を伸ばした状態で
外に座らせられた豚は、
肌色で、その背中はとても大きく、
まるで　何も知らずに
男達を信じて、無邪気に待っている
人間のようでした。

その豚から少し離れた前方で
男達は、微笑みながら話します。
「今年は沢山取れそうだぞ。」
「いくらで売れるかな。」
「知り合いにも分けてやろう。」
豚は男達が何を話しているのか
全く分かりませんでしたが、
その皆のニヤニヤした顔つきが
妙に気になりました。

「さぁ、こっちへ　おいで。」

豚は言われるまま、連れられるまま
部屋に入りました。

ズドン。

ピストルで撃たれました。

ナイフで刺されました。
体は切り刻まれて、血だらけになりました。
豚は死にました。
そして、ハムやソーセージになりました。
私が見たのは以上です。

　　　　　　　　２０１０.２.２７

A Pig That Was Killed

-A Witness' Testimony-

Yes, I saw the incident on the day in question.
The pig was living peacefully as usual.
When the men came to take her,
She went with them without protest
Because they were the ones who gave her food
Everyday.
The pig was made to sit on the ground
In a position that stretched her legs forward.
She was flesh-colour and her back was so broad
That she looked like a person who was waiting for the men.

The men, a little in front of her, were
Talking and smiling.
"We an get a lot for her this year."
"How much do you think we can sell her for?"
"I'll give my friend some of it."
The pig was suddenly concerned about
Their grinning faces
Although she did not understand
What they were talking about at all.

"Come this way."
The pig was taken to a room and lead in
Just as she was told to do.

Zudon!

She was shot with a pistol,
She was stabbed with a knife.
Her body became mutilated and bloody.
She finally died
And was turned into ham and sausages.

That's what I witnessed.

27 February 2010

青い空の中の単純な幸せ

青い空を眺めて　綺麗だなと感じたり、
カラフルな花の色を見て
素晴らしいなと思ったり、
大好きな烏賊のお寿司を食べて
美味しいなと思えることは
単純だけれど、
本当はとても幸せなことなのだと思う。

死ぬまでの一分一秒
私は何をしているのだろう。
その時、幸せだったと思えるのだろうか。

2010.3.26

Simple Happiness In The Blue Sky

I believe that they are very happy things
Even though they are also simple things;
To feel the blue sky beautiful
When I gaze at it,
To be impressed by the wonderful colors
When I see the colorful flowers,
And to think the sushi delicious
When I have my favorite squid sushi.

I am wondering what I will be doing
One minutes, one second before I pass away.
I am wondering if I will be able to feel that I was happy then.

26 March 2010

人生の秘訣

物事全て
うまくいくも　いかぬも
機転とタイミング

スムーズにいかない時は
あなたの頭がボーッとしている時か
それをする為のその時ではない時

だから、怒ったり
イライラしても始まらない
もっと詰まらなくするだけ
涙は自分を惨めにするだけ

鳴くまで待とう、ホトトギス
人生の秘訣　その1

2010.4.27

Secret In Life

Whether everything goes well or not
Depends on your wit and your timing.
When a thing does not work smoothly,
It must be that you are absent-minded
Or the time is not right to do it.

Therefore, there is no use getting angry or irritated.
It just makes you more annoyed.
Tears just make you miserable.

Wait until Hototogisu sings!
That is the first secret in life.

27 April 2010

小鳥さんのお葬式

ある暑い日
運河にある柳の木の下で
小さなお葬式がありました。
「皆様、本日はご参列頂きまして、
　有難うございました。」
と、喪主が挨拶をして、お葬式は終わりました。

(警察のメモ)
6月16日（水）　17：00〜17：30
　民家の前、イタリアンレストランの入口、
　看板の下などで、母親を探す迷子の小鳥　二羽、
　目撃される

同日　　　21：30〜21：40
　捜査の結果、ある民家付近で、声だけ聞く。
　動物園に保護されたとの噂あり。

6月17日（木）　17：45
　歩道上で、ぺちゃんこになった小鳥の
　遺体一体、発見
　轢き逃げ、死体遺棄の疑い

6月18日（金）　17：00
　葬儀

　　　　　　　　　　　　　2010.6.20

A Chick's Funeral

One hot day
There was a funeral under weeping willows beside a canal.
"Ladies and gentlemen,
I really appreciate your attendance today,"
The chief mourner greeted the visitors.
Then the funeral ended.

(The police officer's note)
Wednesday 16th June, 17:00~17:30,
In front of an Italian restaurant,
Under the sign of the restaurant and so on
Two lost chicks that were looking for their mother were seen.

The same day around 21:30~21:40
As a result of the search,
The voice was heard around a house.
There was a rumor that they were protected by the Zoo.

Thursday 17th June, 17:45,
The flat corpse of a chick was discovered on the street.
Suspicion of a hit-and-run accident.

Friday 8th June, 17:00,
A funeral.

20 June 2010

雪山の遭難者

蜂さん、蜂さん、
どうして雪の上で寝ているの？
凍えて死んでしまうよ。

大きすぎる氷の粒が当たっちゃったの？
強い風が家へ帰る方向を失わせちゃったの？
あそこで寝ているのは、みんな仲間なの？

この雪が溶けたら、
また元気になって飛べるのかな。
今日は綺麗な青い空だね。
お休み、蜂さん達。

２０１０．１２．８

THE VICTIM ON THE SNOWY MOUNTAIN

Hey, bee, bee!
Why are you sleeping on the snow?
You are going to freeze to death!

Were you caught by some grain of ice which was too big for you?
Did you lose your direction in the strong wind?
Are those bees sleeping over there your friends?

I hope that you will be able to recover and fly again.
It is a beautiful blue sky today, isn't it?
Sweet dreams, bees.

8 December 2010

【筆者紹介】

自見　良津枝

福島県出身。日本語教師。詩人。
１９９２年から執筆活動を始める。
１９９５年、東洋大学短期大学部日本文学科卒業。
１９９９年、慶應義塾大学文学部哲学類卒業。
２０００年、英語の教員免許取得。
２００２年、日本語教師養成学校修了後、
　　　　　　カナダでの研修を経て、
　　　　　　日本語教師として働き始める。
現在、アイルランド在住。

【カバー】

写真：コンラド・リナ (http://kestrelofbahji.com)

モデル：スキ

絵画：バージのチョウゲンボウ（コンラド・リナ）

折り紙アートのホームページ：

http://niko-niko-nihongo.com

Poet's Biography

Mitsue Jimi,

Born in Fukushima, Japan.

Japanese language teacher and Poet.

Began writing poetry and fairytales in 1992.

1995: Graduated from Toyo University Junior College, Tokyo.

1999: Bachelor of Arts in Literature, Keio Gijuku University, Tokyo.

2000: Liscenced as an English Teacher.

2002: Certification as a Japanese Teacher, Arc Academy, Tokyo.

2002: Began career as a teacher of Japanese.

Presently teaching Japanese in Dublin, Ireland.

Book cover

Photographer: Conrad Reina (http://kestrelofbahji.com)
Model: Suki
Painting: Kestrel of Bahji by Conrad Reina
Origami art: http://niko-niko-nihongo.com